Standards for K–12 Engineering Education?

Committee on Standards for K–12 Engineering Education

NATIONAL ACADEMY OF ENGINEERING
OF THE NATIONAL ACADEMIES

THE NATIONAL ACADEMIES PRESS
Washington, D.C.
www.nap.edu

NATIONAL ACADEMIES PRESS   500 Fifth Street, N.W.   Washington, DC 20001

NOTICE: This publication has been reviewed according to procedures approved by a National Academy of Engineering report review process. Publication of signed work signifies that it is judged a competent and useful contribution worthy of public consideration, but it does not imply endorsement of conclusions or recommendations by the National Academy of Engineering. The interpretations and conclusions in such publications are those of the authors and do not purport to represent the views of the council, officers, or staff of the National Academy of Engineering.

This study was supported by Contract/Grant No. DRL-0733584 between the National Academy of Sciences and the National Science Foundation. Additional support was provided by the S.D. Bechtel, Jr. Foundation and Parametric Technology Corporation, Inc. Any opinions, findings, conclusions, or recommendations expressed in this publication are those of the author(s) and do not necessarily reflect the views of the organizations or agencies that provided support for the project.

International Standard Book Number 13: 978-0-309-16015-5
International Standard Book Number 10: 0-309-16015-4

Copies of this report are available from National Academies Press, 500 Fifth Street, N.W., Lockbox 285, Washington, DC 20055; (800) 624-6242 or (202) 334-3313 (in the Washington metropolitan area); online at http://www.nap.edu.

Printed in the United States of America

THE NATIONAL ACADEMIES
Advisers to the Nation on Science, Engineering, and Medicine

The **National Academy of Sciences** is a private, nonprofit, self-perpetuating society of distinguished scholars engaged in scientific and engineering research, dedicated to the furtherance of science and technology and to their use for the general welfare. Upon the authority of the charter granted to it by the Congress in 1863, the Academy has a mandate that requires it to advise the federal government on scientific and technical matters. Dr. Ralph J. Cicerone is president of the National Academy of Sciences.

The **National Academy of Engineering** was established in 1964, under the charter of the National Academy of Sciences, as a parallel organization of outstanding engineers. It is autonomous in its administration and in the selection of its members, sharing with the National Academy of Sciences the responsibility for advising the federal government. The National Academy of Engineering also sponsors engineering programs aimed at meeting national needs, encourages education and research, and recognizes the superior achievements of engineers. Dr. Charles M. Vest is president of the National Academy of Engineering.

The **Institute of Medicine** was established in 1970 by the National Academy of Sciences to secure the services of eminent members of appropriate professions in the examination of policy matters pertaining to the health of the public. The Institute acts under the responsibility given to the National Academy of Sciences by its congressional charter to be an adviser to the federal government and, upon its own initiative, to identify issues of medical care, research, and education. Dr. Harvey V. Fineberg is president of the Institute of Medicine.

The **National Research Council** was organized by the National Academy of Sciences in 1916 to associate the broad community of science and technology with the Academy's purposes of furthering knowledge and advising the federal government. Functioning in accordance with general policies determined by the Academy, the Council has become the principal operating agency of both the National Academy of Sciences and the National Academy of Engineering in providing services to the government, the public, and the scientific and engineering communities. The Council is administered jointly by both Academies and the Institute of Medicine. Dr. Ralph J. Cicerone and Dr. Charles M. Vest are chair and vice chair, respectively, of the National Research Council.

www.national-academies.org

COMMITTEE ON STANDARDS FOR K–12 ENGINEERING EDUCATION

ROBERT M. WHITE, NAE (*chair*), Carnegie Mellon University, Palo Alto, California
TODD R. ALLEN, Allen Research, Technologies and Services, Inc., Atlanta, Georgia
CHRISTINE M. CUNNINGHAM, Museum of Science, Boston, Massachusetts
HEIDI A. DIEFES-DUX, Purdue University, West Lafayette, Indiana
MARIO A. GODOY-GONZALEZ, Royal High School, Royal City, Washington
PAMELA B. NEWBERRY, Project Lead the Way, Inc., Wytheville, Virginia
LINDA P. ROSEN, Education and Management Innovations, Inc., Bethesda, Maryland
F. JAMES RUTHERFORD, American Association for the Advancement of Science, Berkeley, California
CHRISTIAN D. SCHUNN, University of Pittsburgh, Pennsylvania
SUSAN K. SCLAFANI, National Center for Education and the Economy, Washington, D.C.
JAMES C. SPOHRER, IBM Almaden Research Center, San Jose, California
ELIZABETH K. STAGE, Lawrence Hall of Science, Berkeley, California
ROBERTA R. TANNER, Loveland High School, Colorado

Project Staff

GREG PEARSON, Study Director and Senior Program Officer, National Academy of Engineering
MARIBETH KEITZ, Senior Program Associate, National Academy of Engineering
CAROL ARENBERG, Senior Editor, National Academy of Engineering

Preface

This report is the final product of a two-year study by the Committee on Standards for K–12 Engineering Education, a group of experts on diverse subjects working under the auspices of the National Academy of Engineering (NAE). The committee's charge was to assess the potential value and feasibility of developing and implementing content standards for engineering education at the K–12 level in the United States. Such standards have been developed for three disciplines in STEM education—science, technology, and mathematics—but not for engineering. In fulfilling its charge, the committee reviewed existing efforts to define what K–12 students should know and be able to do related to engineering; evaluated evidence for the value and impact of content standards in other areas of K–12 education; identified elements of existing standards documents for K–12 science, mathematics, and technology that could link to engineering; and considered how the various purposes for K–12 engineering education might affect the content and implementation of standards.

Historically, in U.S. elementary and secondary schools, the "E" of STEM has been virtually silent. But a small and apparently growing number of efforts are being made to introduce engineering experiences to K–12 students. Given this phenomenon, the emphasis on standards in education reform in this country, and concerns about how well we are preparing students for life and work in the highly technological 21st century, it is reasonable that we focus attention on the need for and value of standards for K–12 engineering education.

This report should be of interest to a variety of audiences, including leaders in the K–12 STEM education community, STEM professional societies, policy makers at the state and federal levels, businesses and industries engaged in K–12 STEM education outreach, individuals and organizations responsible for teacher education and teacher professional development, and developers of curricula, assessments, and textbooks.

The committee met face-to-face three times and many more times by telephone. In addition, the committee sponsored a two-day data-gathering workshop and commissioned six papers on topics relevant to the charge. The report is based on the data gathered through these efforts, as well as on the personal and professional experience and judgments of committee members.

Robert M. White, *Chair*
Committee on Standards for K–12 Engineering Education

Acknowledgments

This report has been reviewed in draft form by individuals chosen for their diverse perspectives and technical expertise, in accordance with procedures approved by the National Academies. The purpose of this independent review is to provide candid and critical comments that will assist the committee and the National Academy of Engineering in making its published report as sound as possible and to ensure that it meets institutional standards for objectivity, evidence, and responsiveness to the study charge. The reviewers' comments and the draft manuscript remain confidential to protect the integrity of the deliberative process. We wish to thank the following individuals for their review of this report:

Rodger Bybee, Rodger Bybee & Associates, and President Emeritus, Biological Sciences Curriculum Study

Howard Gobstein, Executive Officer and Vice President, Research, Innovation and STEM Education, Co-Director, Science and Mathematics Teacher Imperative, Association of Public and Land-Grant Universities

Richard Lehrer, Department of Teaching and Learning, Peabody College, Vanderbilt University

Ioannis Miaoulis, President and CEO, Museum of Science, Boston

Frederic A. Mosher, Senior Research Consultant to the Consortium for Policy Research in Education, Teachers College, Columbia University

Teri Reed-Rhoads, Assistant Dean of Engineering for Undergraduate Education and Associate Professor of Engineering Education, Purdue University

Kendall N. Starkweather, Executive Director/CEO, International Technology and Engineering Education Association

Steven S. Wagner, Engineer Teacher, Highland Science High School, Henrico, Virginia

Robin Willner, Vice President, Global Community Initiatives, IBM Corporation

Although the reviewers listed above have provided many constructive comments and suggestions, they were not asked to endorse the conclusions or recommendations, and they did not see the final draft of the report before its public release. The review of this report was overseen by Linda M. Abriola, Dean of Engineering and Professor of Civil and Environmental Engineering, Tufts University, Boston, Massachusetts. Appointed by the NAE, she was responsible for ensuring that an independent examination of the report was carried out in accordance with institutional procedures and that all review comments were carefully considered. Responsibility for the final content of this report rests entirely with the authoring committee and the institution.

In addition to the reviewers, many other individuals assisted in the development of this report. The committee commissioned six papers to provide a firm grounding in the current status of relevant research and education. Rodger Bybee, Rodger Bybee and Associates, prepared a paper on opportunities and barriers to the development and implementation of standards for K–12 engineering; Rodney L. Custer, Jenny L. Daugherty, and Joseph P. Meyer, Illinois State University, prepared a paper on the conceptual base for secondary-level engineering education; Marc J. De Vries, Eindhoven University of Technology/Delft University of Technology, the Netherlands, prepared a paper on standards for precollege engineering education in countries outside the United States; Jacob Foster, Massachusetts Department of Elementary and Secondary Education, prepared a paper on the history of engineering/technology standards in his state; James Rutherford, a committee member and retired education advisor to the Executive Officer of the American Association for the Advancement of Science, prepared a paper on alternatives to traditional content standards; and Cary Sneider, Portland State University, and committee member Linda Rosen, of Education and Management Innovations, Inc., prepared a paper on how engineering concepts are or might be incorporated into standards for science and mathematics. A number of other thoughtful individuals provided input to the project at the committee's July 2009 workshop.

Thanks are also due to the project staff. Maribeth Keitz managed the committee's logistical and administrative needs and saw to it that meetings and the workshop were run efficiently and smoothly. Carolyn Williams, Christine Mirzayan Science & Technology Policy Graduate Fellow, conducted research on precollege engineering education standards outside the United States; her work led to the commissioning of the paper by Marc J. de Vries. NAE Senior Editor Carol R. Arenberg substantially improved the readability of the report. Greg Pearson, NAE senior program officer, played a key role in conceptualizing the study and managed the project from start to finish.

Contents

APPENDIXES

Executive Summary

The goal of the study described in this executive summary was to assess the value and feasibility of developing and implementing content standards for engineering education at the K–12 level. Content standards have been developed for three disciplines in STEM education—science, technology, and mathematics—but not for engineering. To date, a small but growing number of K–12 students are being exposed to engineering-related materials, and limited but intriguing evidence suggests that engineering education can stimulate interest and improve learning in mathematics and science as well as improve understanding of engineering and technology. Given this background, a reasonable question is whether standards would improve the quality and increase the amount of teaching and learning of engineering in K–12 education.

Overall Conclusion

The committee concluded that, although it is theoretically possible to develop standards for K–12 engineering education, it would be extremely difficult to ensure their usefulness and effective implementation. This conclusion is supported by the following findings: (1) there is relatively limited experience with K–12 engineering education in U.S. elementary and secondary schools, (2) there is not at present a critical mass of teachers qualified to deliver engineering instruction, (3) evidence regarding the impact of standards-based educational reforms on student learning in other subjects, such as mathematics and science, is inconclusive, and (4) there are significant barriers to introducing stand-alone standards for an entirely new content area in a curriculum already burdened with learning goals in more established domains of study.

Alternatives to New Standards

For all of the reasons described above, the committee argues against the development of standards for K–12 engineering education at this time. Instead, we urge two approaches for leveraging current national and state standards to improve the quality of K–12 engineering education in the United States.

The first approach, infusion, is a proactive strategy to embed relevant learning goals from one discipline (e.g., engineering) into standards for another (e.g., mathematics). This could be done most easily when state or national standards are being revised. The second approach, mapping, would involve integrating (or mapping) "big ideas" in engineering onto current standards in other disciplines. Mapping is a strategy for retrospectively drawing attention to connections that may or may not have been recognized by the developers of current standards.

Core Ideas in Engineering

Both infusion and mapping will require consensus on the most important concepts, skills, and habits of mind in engineering. Agreement on these core ideas may be thought of as a first step in the development of standards, but it does not necessarily lead to the development of full-fledged standards. Even if standards for engineering education are never developed, the core ideas will benefit curriculum developers, cognitive scientists, teachers, those working in informal and after-school learning environments, and others. Although a number of groups have tried to articulate core ideas, a more rigorous and inclusive process will be necessary to achieve formal consensus.

RECOMMENDATION 1. Federal agencies, foundations, and professional engineering societies with an interest in improving precollege engineering education should fund a consensus process to develop a document describing the core ideas of engineering that are appropriate for K–12 students. The process should include the views of a wide range of stakeholders. Work should begin as soon as possible, and the findings should be shared with key audiences, including developers of new or revised standards in science, mathematics, engineering, and technology at the national and state levels.

Guidelines for the Development of Instructional Materials

One important benefit of core ideas would be to support the development of guidelines for K–12 engineering instructional materials. Guidelines would help curriculum developers focus these materials on the core ideas and ensure that students would be exposed to materials representative of the actual practice of engineering. Thus guidelines could have an immediate, positive effect on the development of K–12 engineering curricula.

RECOMMENDATION 2. The U.S. Department of Education and National Science Foundation should jointly fund the development of guidelines for K–12 engineering instructional materials. Development should be overseen by an organization with expertise in K–12 education policy in concert with the engineering community. Other partners should include mathematics, science, technology education, social studies, and English-language-arts teacher professional societies; curriculum development and teacher professional development experts; and organizations representing informal and after-school education. Funding should be sufficient for an initial, intense development effort that lasts for one year or less, and additional support should be provided for periodic revisions as more research data become available about learning and teaching engineering on the K–12 level.

Research on Learning

The committee found very little research by cognitive scientists that could inform the development of standards for engineering education in K–12. This was also the finding of the Committee on K–12 Engineering Education, which authored *Engineering in K–12 Education: Understanding the Status and Improving the Prospects*, a 2009 report by the National Academies. We suggest that the previous committee's recommendations related to research on learning be (1) evaluated for their relevance to the infusion and mapping approaches described in this report and (2) expanded.

RECOMMENDATION 3. The following research questions should be part of a wide-ranging research agenda in K–12 engineering education funded by the National Science Foundation, other federal agencies, and the private sector:

- How do children come to understand (or misunderstand) core concepts and apply (or misapply) skills in engineering?
- What are the most effective ways of introducing and sequencing engineering concepts and skills for learners at the elementary, middle, and high school levels?
- What are the most important synergies in the learning and teaching of engineering and mathematics, science, technology, and other subjects?
- What are the most important considerations in designing materials, programs, assessments, and educator professional development that engage all learners, including those historically underrepresented in engineering?
- What are the best settings and strategies for enabling young people to understand engineering in schools, informal education institutions, and after-school programs?

Impact of Reforms

Although measuring the impact of reform efforts in K–12 education can be very difficult, the committee concluded that assessing the effects of the infusion and mapping approaches, core ideas, and guidelines for instructional materials will be essential for the development of K–12 engineering education in the United States over time. Data from these assessments will also provide a basis for evaluating the efficacy of continuing to pursue these and related efforts.

RECOMMENDATION 4. Federal agencies with an interest in improving STEM education should support a large-scale survey to establish a comprehensive picture of K–12 engineering education nationally and at the state level. The survey should encompass formal and informal education, including after-school initiatives; build on data collected in the recent National Academies report on K–12 engineering education; and be conducted by an experienced education research organization. The survey should be periodically repeated to measure changes in the quality, scale, and impact of K–12 engineering education, and it should specifically take into account how the practices of infusion and mapping, consensus on core ideas in engineering, and the development of guidelines for instructional materials have contributed to change.

A Final Word

Although the committee concluded that content standards for K–12 engineering education are not now warranted, our enthusiasm for the potential value of engineering education to our country's young people and, ultimately, to the nation as a whole has not been diminished. For a country like the United States, which is largely dependent on technological development, we can think of few areas of education as critical as engineering to building an informed, literate citizenry; ensuring our quality of life; and addressing the serious challenges facing our country and the world.

1

Introduction

This report comes at a time of widespread interest in improving science, technology, engineering, and mathematics (STEM) education in elementary and secondary schools. STEM education at the K–12 level is important in part because it can develop student interest and aptitude in subjects directly relevant to the nation's capacity for research and innovation. This capacity is largely credited with supporting U.S. economic health, national security, and quality of life (NAS, NAE, and IOM, 2007). More generally, K–12 STEM education contributes to scientific and technological literacy, important attributes for all citizens.

President Barack Obama has made STEM education a priority for his administration (Obama, 2009), and policy changes and funding have followed. The U.S. Department of Education has more than $4.3 billion to support the Race to the Top Fund, an initiative that includes incentives for states to improve STEM teaching and learning (DOEd, 2009). The White House is also backing Educate to Innovate, a major public-private initiative that will bring additional resources and attention to STEM education (Chang, 2009).

At the same time, a coalition led by the National Governors Association and the Council of Chief State School Officers has embarked on an effort to create common standards in core subjects, including mathematics (*www.corestandards.org*). The hope is that states will adopt the standards, thereby making curricula, assessments, and teacher professional development more consistent and more rigorous and, ultimately, raising student achievement. In addition, the National Research Council (NRC) is developing a content framework for the next generation of science standards. A draft of the framework released for public comment in July 2010 included a section devoted to engineering and technology.

Motivated by concerns that too few U.S. students are interested in or performing at high enough levels in STEM subjects (e.g., Carnegie Corporation of New York, 2009), foundations and businesses are supporting efforts by several states that are restructuring or are planning to substantially restructure their K–12 STEM education systems (e.g., *www.ncstem.org*, *www.osln.org*, *www.californiastem.org*).

Historically, the "T" and, especially, the "E" in STEM have not received the same level of attention as the "S" and "M." The "T," technology education (and its predecessors industrial and manual arts), have a long history (Herschbach, 2009), a small but dedicated teacher corps (Dugger, 2007), and, as of 2000, a set of standards specifying what students should know and be able to do to be considered technologically literate. These standards include engineering-related learning goals. In fact, based on the shift in technology education toward engineering, ITEA (International Technology Education Association) members voted in early 2010 to change the name of their organization to the International Technology and Engineering Educators Association (ITEEA).

In contrast, the "E," engineering education, has only recently begun to make its way into the K–12 classroom. According to a recent estimate, some 5 million K–12 students have taken part in formal engineering curricula since the early 1990s (NAE and NRC, 2009). Although this is a small number compared with the roughly 56 million students enrolled annually in K–12 schools (DOEd, 2008), it indicates that STEM education is expanding beyond science and mathematics. K–12 students are also being exposed to engineering in informal settings—such as after-school programs and visits to informal-education institutions, such as museums and science centers. For example, some 160,000 students ages 6 to 18 participated in engineering-related design competitions through the FIRST program (FIRST, 2009).

Developers of engineering curricula, informal and after-school engineering programs, engineering professional societies, a number of engineering schools and companies, and a growing cadre of education researchers and teachers believe engineering education offers K–12 students a number of benefits, including stimulating interest and improving achievement in mathematics and science, developing engineering design skills, increasing technological literacy, improving the understanding of engineering and the work of engineers, and attracting young people to careers in engineering.

Evidence of these benefits is slim so far, in large part because few rigorous impact studies have been conducted. However, as was noted in *Engineering in K–12 Education: Understanding the Status and Improving the Prospects*, the data are strongest for the potential positive impact of engineering on the learning of mathematics and science (NAE and NRC, 2009). In fact, the report found that enhancing the study of science and mathematics for all students—the "mainline"—was the most common objective of existing K–12 engineering curricula. Only a few had as their primary purpose preparing students to pursue careers in engineering or other technical fields, often referred to as the engineering or STEM "pipeline."[1]

However, K–12 engineering education is being taught in the absence of content standards to define what students should know and be able to do, even though standards have been a major element in education reform in the United States for more than 20 years. Existing standards in other subjects, such as science and technology education, do include connections to engineering, but there are no separate, comprehensive, grade-by-grade standards for engineering in K–12 education.

Defining Engineering

Engineering has been defined as design under constraints (Wulf, 1998), and the most fundamental of these constraints is the laws of nature. Engineers designing a solution to a particular problem must, for example, take into account how physical objects behave in motion. Other constraints include time, money, available materials, ergonomics, environmental regulations, manufacturability, reparability, and political considerations.

Engineers design with the goal of meeting human needs and wants. Design is an iterative process that begins with the identification of a problem and ends with a solution that takes into

---

[1] It is probably more accurate to describe the track followed by STEM students as "pathways," since there are multiple routes into and out of careers. However, for the purposes of contrasting the general-education and engineering-preparation purposes of K–12 engineering education, the committee has chosen to use the mainline-pipeline metaphor.

account the identified constraints and meets specifications for desired performance. Because engineering design problems do not have single, correct solutions, engineering, by necessity, is a creative endeavor. Indeed, while scientists are most concerned with discovering what is, engineers are concerned with what might be. In addition to constraints and specifications, other important ideas in engineering are: systems, modeling, predictive analysis, optimization, and trade-offs. Although each of these terms has a general meaning, in the context of engineering the meanings are often specific. For instance, engineers use modeling to understand how a product or component may function when in use. Models can be drawings or constructed physical objects, such as mock-ups of an airfoil made from plastic or wood or mathematical representations that can be used to predict and study the behavior of a design before it is constructed.

Engineering has strong connections to many other disciplines, particularly mathematics and science. Engineers use science and mathematics in their work, and scientists and mathematicians use the products of engineering—technology—in theirs. Engineers use mathematics to describe and analyze data and, as noted, to develop models for evaluating design solutions. Engineers must also be knowledgeable about science—typically physics, biology, or chemistry—that is relevant to the problem they are engaged in solving. Sometimes, research conducted by engineers results in new scientific discoveries. For a more complete discussion of the origins and nature of engineering, see NAE and NRC (2009, chapter 2, "What Is Engineering?").

A Brief History of Standards in STEM Education[2]

Educational standards are not new. More than a century ago, the Committee of Ten, a working group of educators assembled by the National Education Association, recommended requirements for college admissions, including laboratory experience. The committee's report influenced numerous programs and practices in the nation's high schools (DeBoer, 1991; Sizer, 1964). For instance, it was the impetus for the Harvard Descriptive List, a set of 40 physics experiments students applying to the college were required to complete. Applicants also had to take a written test about the experiments and principles of physics. In essence, the list, which defined a combination of content and teaching goals, was a set of standards.

Since the late 1800s, numerous policies, generally in the form of committee reports, have described what we now call educational standards. In the late 1980s, a new stage of education, the "standards era," emerged. The origins of this new era can be traced back to *A Nation at Risk*, a report by the National Commission on Excellence in Education (NCEE, 1983), which included high school graduation requirements in five core subjects—English, mathematics, science, social studies, and computer science. The report also included two recommendations for strengthening the content of the core curriculum and using measurable goals to assess progress in learning. These requirements set the stage for standards as we know them today.

In 1989, then President George H.W. Bush met with governors from across the nation in Charlottesville, Virginia, for an education summit, the outcomes of which laid the groundwork for the Goals 2000 Education Program. The creation of those goals led to initiatives for voluntary national standards in all core subjects. That same year, the National Council of Teachers of Mathematics (NCTM) published *Curriculum and Evaluation Standards for School Mathematics* (NCTM, 1989), and the American Association for the Advancement of Science (AAAS) pub-

---

[2] This section is based in part on a commissioned paper prepared for the committee by Rodger Bybee, Rodger Bybee and Associates. For the complete paper, see p. 55, Appendix B.

lished *Science for All Americans* (AAAS, 1989). Both publications supported further standards-based reform.

There are three generally accepted reasons for adopting educational standards: to ensure quality, to define goals, and to promote change (NCTM, 1989). Standards are also often considered to be statements of equity, that is, the expectations they express pertain to *all* students (e.g., NRC, 1996; Schoenfeld, 2002). This report focuses on content standards, though several other types of standards have been developed (Box 1-1).

BOX 1-1
Types of Educational Standards

Content Standards—a description of the knowledge and skills students are expected to have mastered by the end of their schooling. Content standards describe learning outcomes, but they are *not* instructional materials (i.e., lessons, classes, courses of study, or school programs).

Teaching Standards—a description of the educational experiences that should be provided by teachers, textbooks, and educational technology. Teaching standards relate to the quality of instruction and sometimes emphasize unique features, such as the use of integrated instructional sequences.

Teacher Professional Development Standards—a description of subject-specific and pedagogical knowledge and skills teachers are expected to attain through professional development experiences. These standards provide guidelines for all parties involved in teacher preparation, including schools of education and policy makers who determine requirements for teacher certification.

Program Standards—criteria for the quality of school education programs. Program standards are guidelines for designing programs, in keeping with content, teaching, and assessment standards, and descriptions of the conditions necessary to ensure that all students have appropriate learning experiences.

Assessment Standards—requirements for assessments used to measure student achievement and opportunities to learn. Assessment standards provide guidelines for teachers and state and federal agencies designing assessment tasks, practices, and policies.

Performance Standards—a description of the form and function of achievement that show what students have learned. Performance standards, usually described in relation to content standards, sometimes identify levels of achievement for content standards (e.g., basic, proficient, advanced).

The fundamental idea of standards-based reform was to establish clear, coherent, and important content as learning outcomes for K–12 education. Funders and developers assumed that voluntary national standards would be used by state education departments and local jurisdictions to select educational programs, guide instructional practices, and implement assessments that would help students attain the standards. They also assumed that undergraduate teacher education and professional development for classroom teachers would be aligned with standards. These assumptions sound straightforward, but the reality has been considerably more complex. Because of the many independent decisions affecting teacher preparation, curriculum, and testing, the influence of national standards on teaching and learning has been highly variable (NRC, 2001). This issue is discussed more fully in Chapter 2.

In the two decades since the release of *Science for All Americans* (AAAS, 1989), a number of other STEM-related standards initiatives have been undertaken. In 1991, *What Work Requires of Schools*, a report of the Secretary's Commission for Achieving Necessary Skills (DOL, 1991), and *Professional Standards for Teaching Mathematics*, an NCTM report, were both published. In 1993, building on *Science for All Americans*, AAAS published *Benchmarks for Science Literacy*, followed in 1996 by the NRC's *National Science Education Standards*. In 2000, ITEA released *Standards for Technological Literacy: Content for the Study of Technology*, and NCTM published its revised standards in *Principles and Standards for School Mathematics*. A third NCTM revision, *Curriculum Focal Points for Prekindergarten through Grade 8*, was published in 2008. Today, as noted earlier, an initiative is under way to develop common core standards in mathematics and science. (For a more detailed chronology of STEM-related standards initiatives in the past 40 years, see the annex to this chapter.)

Project Goal, Objectives, and Study Process

The goal of the project described in this report was to assess the potential value and feasibility of developing and implementing content standards for K–12 engineering education. The project committee was not asked to develop standards for K–12 engineering and did not attempt to do so. The committee's statement of task included the following objectives:

1. Review existing efforts to define what K–12 students should know and be able to do related to engineering, both in the United States and other nations.
2. Evaluate the evidence for the value and impact of content standards in K–12 education.
3. Identify elements of existing standards documents for K–12 science, mathematics, and technology that could link to engineering.
4. Consider how the various possible purposes for K–12 engineering education might affect the content and implementation of standards.
5. Suggest what changes to educational policies, programs, and practices at the national and state levels might be needed to develop and successfully implement K–12 engineering standards or alternative approaches to standardizing the content of K–12 engineering education.

To address these objectives, the committee conducted a variety of information-gathering activities, including commissioning papers on relevant topics (see Appendix B), soliciting input from experts at a two-day workshop in summer 2009 (the workshop agenda appears at Appendix C), and conducting additional research. The committee had three face-to-face meetings (including the workshop) and eight project-related conference calls. Additional input was received from the report reviewers (listed on p. ix), whose task was to ensure that the report addresses the statement of task.

Content of the Report and Intended Audience

This report includes an executive summary, four chapters, and several appendixes. Chapter 2 provides a discussion of the arguments for and against developing content standards for engineering in K–12 education. In Chapter 3, the committee describes how current standards in other subjects may be leveraged to improve the quality and consistency of K–12 engineering education. Chapter 4 provides the committee's conclusions and recommendations. Appendix A provides biographical information about committee members, Appendix B contains the commissioned papers, and Appendix C has the agenda for the July 2009 workshop.

This report should be of interest to a varied audience, including leaders in the K–12 STEM education community, STEM professional societies, policy makers at the state and federal levels, business and industry engaged in K–12 STEM education outreach, individuals and institutions responsible for teacher education and teacher professional development, and developers of curricula, assessments, and textbooks.

References

AAAS (American Association for the Advancement of Science). 1989. Science for All Americans: A Project 2061 Report on Literacy Goals in Science, Mathematics, and Technology. Washington, DC: AAAS.

AAAS. 1993. Benchmarks for Science Literacy. Project 2061. Washington, DC: AAAS.

Carnegie Corporation of New York. 2009. The Opportunity Equations: Transforming Mathematics and Science Education for Citizenship and the Global Economy. Institute for Advanced Study, Commission on Mathematics and Science Education. Available online at *http://www.opportunityequation.org/TheOpportunityEquation.pdf.* (January 26, 2010)

Chang, K. 2009. White House begins campaign to promote science and mathematics education. New York Times. November 23, 2009. Available online at *http://www.nytimes.com/2009/11/24/science/24educ.html.* (January 25, 2010)

DeBoer, G. 1991. A History of Ideas in Science Education. New York: Teachers College Press.

DOEd (U.S. Department of Education). 2008. National Center for Education Statistics. Digest of Education Statistics, 2007 (NCES 2008-022), Table 3. Available online at *http://nces.ed.gov/fastfacts/display.asp?id=65.* (January 26, 2010)

DOEd. 2009. Race to the Top Fund Executive Summary. November 2009. Available online at *http://www2.ed.gov/programs/racetothetop/executive-summary.pdf.* (January 25, 2010)

DOL (U.S. Department of Labor). 1991. What Work Requires of Schools—A SCANS Report for American 2000. Secretary's Commission on Achieving Necessary Skills. Available online at *http://wdr.doleta.gov/SCANS/whatwork/whatwork.pdf.* (January 26, 2010)

Dugger, W.E. Jr. 2007. The status of technology education in the United States: A triennial report of the findings from the states. The Technology Teacher 67(1): 14–21.

FIRST (For Inspiration and Recognition of Science and Technology). 2009. 2008 Annual Report. Available online at *http://www.usfirst.org/uploadedFiles/Who/Annual_Report-Financials/2008_AR_FINAL.pdf.* (January 26, 2010)

Herschbach, D.R. 2009. Technology Education—Foundations and Perspectives. Homewood, IL: American Technical Publishers, Inc.

ITEA (International Technology Education Association). 2000. Standards for Technological Literacy: Content for the Study of Technology. Reston, VA: ITEA.

Kendall, J.S., and R.J. Marzano. 2010. Content knowledge: A compendium of standards and benchmarks for K-12 education. Denver, CO: Mid-continent Research for Education and Learning. 4th ed. Available online at *http://www.mcrel.org/standards-benchmarks/.* (September 13, 2010)

NAE and NRC (National Academy of Engineering and National Research Council). 2009. Engineering in K–12 Education: Understanding the Status and Improving the Prospects. Washington, DC: National Academies Press.

NAS, NAE, and IOM (National Academy of Sciences, National Academy of Engineering, and Institute of Medicine). 2007. Rising Above the Gathering Storm: Energizing and Employing America for a Brighter Economic Future. Washington, DC: National Academies Press.

NCEE (National Commission on Excellence in Education). 1983. A Nation at Risk. Washington, DC: U.S. Government Printing Office.

NCTM (National Council of Teachers of Mathematics). 1989. Curriculum and Evaluation Standards for School Mathematics. Reston, VA: NCTM.

NCTM. 1991. Professional Standards for Teaching Mathematics. Reston, VA: NCTM

NCTM. 2000. Principles and Standards for School Mathematics. Reston, VA: NCTM.

NCTM. 2008. Curriculum Focal Points for Prekindergarten through Grade 8. Reston, VA: NCTM.

NRC (National Research Council). 1996. National Science Education Standards. Washington, DC: National Academy Press.

NRC. 2001. Investigating the Influence of Standards: A Framework for Research in Mathematics, Science, and Technology Education. Committee on Understanding the Influence of Standards in K–12 Science, Mathematics, and Technology Education. Washington, DC: National Academies Press.

Obama, B. 2009. Remarks by the president at the National Academy of Sciences Annual Meeting. April 27, 2009. Washington, D.C. Available online at *http://www.whitehouse.gov/the_press_office/Remarks-by-the-President-at-the-National-Academy-of-Sciences-Annual-Meeting/.* (January 25, 2010)

Schoenfeld, A.H. 2002. Making mathematics work for all children: issues of standards, testing, and equity. Educational Researcher 31: 13–25.

Sizer, T. 1964. Secondary Schools at the Turn of the Century. New Haven, CT: Yale University Press.

Wulf, W.A. 1998. Diversity in engineering. The Bridge 28(4). Available online at http://www.nae.edu/Publications/TheBridge/Archives/CompetitiveMaterialsandSolutions/DiversityinEngineering.aspx. (Accessed May 19, 2010)

ANNEX

Timeline of Selected National Standards Efforts in Mathematics, Science, and Technology[3,4]

1980   *Agenda for Action*, published by the National Council of Teachers of Mathematics (NCTM).

1983   *A Nation at Risk* (NCEE), call for reform of the U.S. education system.

1983   Bill Honig, newly elected state superintendent of California public schools, begins a decade-long revision of the state public school system, the development of curriculum frameworks (content standards) with aligned assessments, professsional development, and instructional materials.

1985   The American Association for the Advancement of Science (AAAS) establishes Project 2061, with the goal of making all Americans scientifically literate. Children beginning school this year, when Halley's Comet was visible from Earth, will see the comet again in 2061, a reasonable time frame for the ambitious goals of Project 2061. The National Council on Science and Technology Education, an independent committee, is established to oversee the project.

1985   *California Mathematics Framework* emphasizes "mathematical power" and problem solving.

1987   NCTM writing teams begin reviewing curricular documents and draft standards for curricula and evaluations.

1989   Publication of *Everybody Counts*, a report of the National Academies' Mathematical Sciences Education Board

1989   The nation's 50 governors, led by Bill Clinton of Arkansas and President G.H.W. Bush, adopt National Education Goals for the year 2000. One goal is that the United States will be "first in the world in mathematics and science."

1989   Publication of *Curriculum and Evaluation Standards for School Mathematics*, a report by NCTM.

1989   Publication by Project 2061 of *Science for All Americans*, which describes the "understandings and habits of mind . . . essential for all citizens in a scientifically literate society." "Science" includes mathematics, science, and the designed world.

1990   In his State of the Union address, President G. H. W. Bush announces the National Education Goals for the year 2000. Shortly thereafter, he and Congress establish a National Education Goals Panel (NEGP).

1990   The Secretary's Commission on Achieving Necessary Skills (SCANS) is appointed by the secretary of labor to determine the skills young people need to succeed in the world of work.

1990   National Educational Assessment of Progress (NAEP) introduces State Mathematics Framework, based on a "content by mathematical ability" matrix grounded in the NCTM *Curriculum and Evaluation Standards*, and begins short-term trend

---

[3] Adapted by permission of McREL from Content Knowledge: A Compendium of Standards and Benchmarks for K–12 Education, *http://www.mcrel.org/standards-benchmarks/docs/purpose.asp*. All rights reserved. Source: Kendall and Marzano, 2010.

[4] Unless the month is specified, the order of entries within years has not been verified.

lines.

1990   Publication of California *Science Framework*, which incorporates ideas from *Science for All Americans*.

1990   The New Standards Project, a joint project of the National Center on Education and the Economy and the Learning Research and Development Center, is formed to create a system of standards and assessments for student performance in literacy, mathematics, science, and applied learning.

1991   SCANS publishes *What Work Requires of Schools*, which describes the knowledge and skills necessary for success in the workplace.

1991   Secretary of Education Lamar Alexander asks Congress to establish the National
(June)   Council on Education Standards and Testing (NCEST) to provide a vehicle for reaching bipartisan consensus on national standards and testing.

1991   NCTM publishes *Professional Standards for Teaching Mathematics*.

1991   NAEP publishes *Science Framework* based on state frameworks and *Science for All Americans*; used for NAEP science assessments in 1996, 2000, and 2005.

1991   The National Science Foundation (NSF) begins to fund State Systemic Initiatives based on the NCTM *Standards* and the "emerging national science education standards."

1992   NCEST releases *Raising Standards for American Education* to Congress, proposing
(Jan.)   the establishment of an oversight board, the National Education Standards and Assessment Council (NESAC), to certify content and performance standards, as well as "criteria" for assessments.

1992   The National Research Council (NRC), with major funding from the U.S. Department of Education and NSF, establishes the National Committee on Science Education Standards and Assessment (NCSESA) to oversee standards development in content, teaching, and assessment.

1993   AAAS Project 2061 publishes *Benchmarks for Science Literacy*.

1993   NCTM publishes *Assessment Standards for School Mathematics*.

1993   NEGP Technical Planning Group issues "Promises to Keep: Creating High
(Nov.)   Standards for American Students" (referred to as the Malcolm Report) calling for the development of a National Education Standards and Improvement Council (NESIC), which would give voluntary national standards a stamp of approval.

1994   President Clinton signs Goals 2000: Educate America Act into law. The legislation
(March)   creates the National Education Standards and Improvement Council (NESIC) to certify national and state content and performance standards, opportunity-to-learn standards, and state assessments; adds two new goals to the national education goals; brings to nine the number of areas for which students should demonstrate "competency over challenging subject matters." The subject areas now covered include foreign languages, the arts, economics, and civics and government.

1994   The International Technology Education Association (ITEA) forms the Technology
(Sept.)   for All American's Project, which begins development of *Rationale and Structure for the Study of Technology*. The first in a series of three documents, this publication makes the case for the importance of technological literacy and paves the way for the development of technological literacy standards.

1995   The New Standards Project releases *Performance Standards*, a three-volume "con-
(Nov.)   sultation draft" for English language arts, mathematics, science, and "applied learn-

	ing," based on NCTM and anticipated NRC standards.
1996 (Jan.)	NRC publishes *National Science Education Standards*, including standards for teaching, professional development, assessment, content, science programs, and systems.
1996 (March)	Governors and business, education and community leaders meet for a National Education Summit that aims to establish high academic standards, assessment, and accountability and improve the use of school technology as a tool to reach high standards. The summit leads to the creation of Achieve, Inc.
1996	ITEA's *Rationale and Structure* document is published, supported by an NSF grant and the National Aeronautics and Space Administration. This document provides a foundational guide for the development of standards in technological literacy.
1997 (Feb.)	President Clinton, in his State of the Union Address, calls on every state to adopt high national standards and declares, "By 1999, every state should test every 4th grader in reading and every 8th grader in math to make sure these standards are met."
1998	AAAS Project 2061 publishes *Blueprints for Reform.*
1998	The Council for Basic Education publishes *Standards For Excellence in Education*, which includes standards in science, history, geography, English language arts, mathematics, civics, foreign language, and the arts.
2000	ITEA publishes *Standards for Technological Literacy: Content for the Study of Technology*, which had been revised four times after three public reviews and reviews by the NRC Standards Review and Technical Review committees and the National Academy of Engineering Special Review Committee.
2000	International Society for Technology in Education (ISTE) publishes *National Educational Technology Standards for Students: Connecting Curriculum and Technology.*
2000	NCTM publishes *Principles and Standards for School Mathematics.*
2000	NRC publishes *Inquiry and the National Science Education Standards: A Guide for Teaching and Learning.*
2001	AAAS Project 2061 publishes *Designs for Science Literacy.*
2001	AAAS Project 2061 publishes *Atlas of Science Literacy*, Vol. 1.
2001	NRC publishes *Classroom Assessment and the National Science Education Standards.*
2005	Revised mathematics framework for state NAEP developed after a period of public comment.
2006	NCTM publishes *Curriculum Focal Points for Prekindergarten through Grade 8 Mathematics.*
2007	AAAS Project 2061 publishes *Atlas of Science Literacy*, Vol. 2.
2007	NAEP *Science Framework* approved for 2009 assessment, the first time Project 2061 *Benchmarks* and NRC *National Science Education Standards* have been incorporated.
2009	NCTM publishes *Focus in High School Mathematics: Reasoning and Sense Making.*
2010 (June)	Release of common core standards for English language arts and mathematics by the National Governors Association and Council of Chief State School Officers.
2010 (winter)	The National Research Council is expected to publish its framework for a new generation of science standards.

2

Arguments For and Against Content Standards for K–12 Engineering Education

This chapter presents the arguments for and against the development and implementation of content standards for K–12 engineering education. However, to make sense of the arguments, one must first understand the nature of existing content standards for other school subjects. Content standards describe subject-specific knowledge, skills, and dispositions that elementary and secondary students are expected to have mastered at different points in their educational careers. These expectations are usually expressed in grade bands, such as kindergarten–grade 2, grades 3–5, grades 6–8, and grades 9–12.

Ideally, content standards draw on studies in the cognitive sciences showing the development of conceptual understanding. Also ideally, standards support the progressive development of conceptual understanding, dispositions, and skills across grades and make explicit connections between related concepts. Researchers have been working to tease out such learning progressions in science education (e.g., Corcoran et al., 2009), but the committee is unaware of this kind of research in K–12 engineering education.

In reality, however, evidence about the nature and progression of learning is far from complete. Even though more data are available to guide standards development now than were available 20 or even 10 years ago, there are still gaps, especially in school subjects as new as engineering. To address these gaps, standards developers typically rely on the expert judgment of teachers, curriculum developers, and others with direct experience with students in the classroom.

It is important to remember that standards differ from the curriculum, which can be summarized as the scope and sequence of teaching and learning in the classroom. The curriculum is informed by standards. As described in Box 1-1, content standards also differ from program standards, assessment standards, and standards for professional development.

In addition, the implementation of standards in individual classrooms does not always match the vision of the original developers. Sometimes less material is covered than is described in the standards. Sometimes more material is covered. In addition, the material that is tested—which is sometimes synonymous with what is considered important—may be only part of what has been taught.

Historically in the United States, content standards have been developed through a consensus process at the national level by coalitions of organizations and individuals with interests and expertise in the subject area. As noted by Bybee (2009), given sufficient resources, expertise, and time, content standards can be developed for any school subject. Based on the committee's experience, the development of de novo, single-subject standards for a K–12 school subject, such as science, mathematics, or technology, requires several million dollars over a period of three to five years.[1]

These content standards development efforts, however, have generally not been associated with a plan or commitment for nationwide implementation. Instead, implementation of national standards begins when states create their own standards, based to varying degrees on the national documents. Because each state has its own educational system, history, and policies, state standards vary considerably in their fidelity to the national documents, as well as in their alignment to one another (Porter et al., 2008). This variability creates a number of challenges related to the quality, consistency, and rigor of what is taught, learned, and assessed (e.g., Finn et al., 2006) and is a major driver of the current movement to establish common standards for core subjects (Box 2-1).

BOX 2-1
Common Core Standards

Forty-eight states, two territories, and the District of Columbia have signaled their support for the common core standards initiative (*www.corestandards.org*), led by the National Governors Association (NGA) and Council of Chief State School Officers (CCSSO) and funded largely by the Bill and Melinda Gates Foundation. Draft standards for K–12 English language arts and mathematics, developed by experts affiliated with Achieve, Inc., ACT, and the College Board, were released for public comment in spring 2010. Supporters of the common core approach hope the new standards will increase the rigor and decrease the number and variability of learning expectations for students.

Participating states are also expected to sign on to the development of common assessments, and the U.S. Department of Education has pledged $350 million to help develop them. It is not clear, however, how these assessments would be designed or whether states will agree to use a common set of measures to judge student performance. A central tension in the project is whether the push for consistency at the national level fundamentally infringes on the tradition of state independence in education decision making.

Some have speculated that science will be the next school subject to become part of the common core standards. Because the draft framework for the next generation of science standards being developed by the National Research Council includes key concepts in engineering and technology, it is possible those subjects may also become part of the common core. When finalized in the first quarter of 2011, the science framework will be handed off to Achieve, Inc., which will use it to create new standards. The decision to include science in the common core standards likely rests with NGA and CCSSO.

---

[1] For example, the *National Science Education Standards* were developed over a period of five years at a cost of $7 million (P. Legro, Koshland Science Museum, personal communication, Feb. 2, 2010).

Education in the United States is a complex system of interacting parts, which in turn is a subsystem of a larger, complex sociopolitical system. Policies at the federal, state, and district levels can influence what happens in the classroom. In addition, business, higher education, and national professional societies also have a stake in K–12 education. Most contemporary theories of education reform suggest that, for standards to have a meaningful impact on student learning, they must be implemented in a way that takes into account the systems nature of education (e.g., AAAS, 1998; NRC, 2002). For example, it is commonly understood that effective standards must be coherently reflected in assessments, curricula, instructional practices, and teacher professional development.

Special Characteristics of K–12 Engineering Education

K–12 engineering education has three important characteristics that must inform standards development and implementation. First, as noted in Chapter 1, compared to other K–12 subjects, engineering has a very small footprint in schools; in addition, almost no undergraduate programs provide training for prospective teachers of engineering. To put it simply, K–12 engineering education is in its infancy, and this has implications for standards.

Second, engineering has strong connections to mathematics, science, and technology, school subjects for which there already are K–12 content standards. In addition, existing standards, particularly for science and technology, exploit their natural connections to engineering. Thus it is reasonable to ask if new engineering standards must include explicit links to these and perhaps other content standards.

Finally, because of the postsecondary, professional track in engineering, some K–12 engineering curricula focus on preparing students to enter engineering schools, sometimes called the "pipeline" approach (e.g., Project Lead the Way, *www.pltw.org*). However, content standards for K–12 school subjects are typically based on a "mainline" goal, that is, general literacy in that field of study. This raises the question of whether there should be two sets of standards for K–12 engineering and, if so, how they might differ.

The Argument for Engineering Content Standards

The feasibility of developing standards depends on two things: (1) time, money, and expertise to accomplish the task; and (2) agreement on the fundamental concepts that underlie the stated learning goals. As to the former, the committee agrees with Bybee (2009) that human and capital resources are not a barrier to standards development. With respect to the latter, one aspect of the study was to review efforts to identify the core content of K–12 engineering. Based on this review, discussed in Chapter 3 and elaborated in an annex to that chapter, the committee believes there is enough agreement about most of the major ideas to suggest that a consensus could be reached through thoughtful, collaborative deliberation.

But the potential value of content standards—in any subject—is not in their development but in their implementation. As a tool for policy change, standards can provide a coherent intellectual framework for reform that can be used in different ways by various groups. For instance, standards can provide guidelines and goals for course designers and teacher educators, even if they do not actually work together. Standards for K–12 engineering education, for example, could inform revisions of existing engineering curricula to align them more closely with essential concepts and practices in engineering and to reflect current findings based on cognitive science. Standards could also inform the creation of new instructional materials and shape engineering teacher education programs.

For a subject new to most K–12 classrooms, standards can also make a statement about the importance of that subject for students and for society at large. Thus standards for K–12 engineering education could help create an identity for engineering as a separate and important discipline in the overall curriculum on a par with more established disciplines. This was an important goal, for example, of the technology education community when it developed the *Standards for Technological Literacy* (ITEA, 2000). Ultimately, standards have the potential to expand the presence of high-quality, rigorous, relevant engineering education for K–12 students.

In working on this project, the committee collected and reviewed information about standards and standards-like documents for precollege engineering education developed by other nations, including Australia, England and Wales, France, Germany, and South Africa (DeVries, 2009; also see Appendix B). Our efforts to draw meaningful inferences for education in the United States were hindered by differences among educational systems and difficulties in finding data on the extent and impact of standards.

The Argument Against Engineering Content Standards

Perhaps the most serious argument against developing content standards for K–12 engineering education is our limited experience with K–12 engineering education in elementary and secondary schools. Although there has been a considerable increase in the last 5 to 10 years, the number of K–12 students, teachers, and schools engaged in engineering education is still extremely small compared to the numbers for almost every other school subject.

For standards to have a chance of succeeding, there must be a critical mass of teachers willing and able to deliver engineering instruction. Although no precise threshold number has been determined, based on the committee's experience with the development of standards in other subjects, 10 percent seems a reasonable minimum. Based on the projected size of the teaching force in 2010 in the U.S. K–12 educational system, this would represent about 380,000 teachers (NCES, 2008), a figure orders of magnitude larger than the estimated K–12 engineering teaching force.

The most recent data available indicate that 40 states have adopted or adapted the *Standards for Technological Literacy*. Of these, 12 require students to take at least one technology education course (Dugger, 2007). It is not clear, however, whether these state standards include the engineering content of the national technological literacy standards. More important, the committee could find no reliable data indicating how many states assess student learning in engineering. Without the pressure of an assessment, particularly an assessment with consequences tied to student performance, teachers may have little incentive to teach engineering.

Another concern is mixed results for nationally developed consensus standards, which have demonstrably influenced the content of state education standards and curricula (e.g., DeBoer, 2006), but have had varying impacts in different states. Overall, this has led to well documented problems of a lack of coherence among standards, instructional practices, assessments and accountability, and teacher professional development (NAEd, 2009; Rothman, 2003). Even when standards influence the content of a curriculum, the material that is actually taught—the enacted curriculum—is influenced much more by teachers' beliefs and experiences than by standards (Spillane, 2004; Weiss et al., 2003).

The underlying assumption of standards-based educational reform is that student learning will be positively affected by standards-related changes. However, the evidence on this point is inconclusive. For example, in a meta-analysis conducted by Harris and Goertz (2008), the authors note that standards that succeed in changing what is taught may do little to change how classroom instruction is delivered. For this reason, they conclude, the impact of standards is frequently not as decisive as advocates hope.

Another concern is that we may not know enough about the teaching and learning of engineering at the K–12 level to develop credible standards. There appears to be a growing convergence on the central importance of the design process in K–12 engineering education; a handful of core ideas, such as constraints, systems, optimization, and trade-offs; and the importance of certain nontechnical skills, such as communication and teamwork. However, almost no research has been done, and there is relatively little practical experience to guide decisions about when specific engineering ideas or concepts should be introduced and at what level of complexity. In addition, opinions differ on how engineering concepts connect with each another and with concepts in mathematics and science. Indeed, standards that encourage separate treatment of engineering may make it more difficult to leverage the connections between engineering, science, and mathematics, potentially reducing the positive effects of engineering on student interest and learning in these domains.

Finally, the prospects for the successful implementation of content standards for K–12 engineering education must be considered in the context of what most educators believe is an overfilled curriculum. Obtaining stakeholder buy-in for a separate, new "silo" of content may be very difficult in this environment, especially because it would probably require eliminating some existing elements of the curriculum to make time and space for engineering.

Conclusion

As a K–12 school subject, engineering is distinct both in terms of its recent appearance in the curriculum and its natural connections to other, more established subjects, particularly science, mathematics, and technology, which already have content standards. Although the main ideas in K–12 engineering education are largely agreed upon, data based on rigorous research on engineering learning at the K–12 level are still not sufficient to develop learning progressions that could be reflected in standards. Even if much more were known about engineering learning, there are legitimate questions about the wisdom of promoting an entirely new silo of content for the K–12 curriculum.

For these reasons, the committee argues against the development of standards for K–12 engineering education at this time. Instead, we suggest other approaches to increasing the presence and improving the quality of K–12 engineering education in the United States. These are discussed in Chapter 3.

References

AAAS (American Association for the Advancement of Science). 1998. Blueprints for Reform: Science, Mathematics, and Technology. Available online at *http://www.project2061.org/ publications/bfr/online/blpintro.htm.* (August 4, 2010)

Bybee, R. 2009. K–12 Engineering Education Standards: Opportunities and Barriers. Paper presented at the NAE Workshop on Standards for K–12 Engineering Education, July 8, 2009, Washington, D.C. Available online at *http://www.nae.edu/Programs/TechLit1/K12stds/ WorkshoponStandardsforK–12EngineeringEducation/15165.aspx.* (January 22, 2010)

Corcoran, T., F.A. Mosher, and A. Rogat. 2009. Learning Progressions in Science: An Evidence-Based Approach to Reform. Consortium for Policy Research in Education (CPRE). CPRE Research Report #RR-63. Philadelphia, PA: CPRE.

DeBoer, G. 2006. History of the science standards movement in the United States. Pp. 7–49 in The Impact of State and National Standards on K–12 Science Teaching, D. Sunal and E. Wright, eds. Charlotte, NC: Information Age Publishing.

DeVries, M.J. 2009. Report for NAE on non-U.S. Standards for Pre-university Engineering Education. Paper presented at the NAE Workshop on Standards for K–12 Engineering Education, July 8, 2009, Washington, D.C. Available online at *http://www.nae.edu/ File.aspx?id=15169.* (January 22, 2010)

Dugger, W.E. Jr. 2007. The status of technology education in the United States: a triennial report of the findings from the states. The Technology Teacher 67(1): 14–21.

Finn, C., L Julian, and M.J. Petrilli. 2006. The State of State Standards—2006. Thomas B. Fordham Foundation. Available online at *http://www.edexcellence.net/doc/State%20of% 20State%20Standards2006FINAL.pdf.* (accessed March 10, 2010)

Harris, D.N., and M. Goertz. 2008. The potential effects of "high-quality and uniform" standards: Lessons from a synthesis of previous research and proposals for a new research agenda. A Final Report to the National Research Council. Available online at *http:// www7.nationalacademies.org/cfe/Harris%20Goertz%20Paper.pdf.* (accessed May 19, 2010)

ITEA (International Technology Education Association). 2000. Standards for Technological Literacy: Content for the Study of Technology. Reston, VA.: ITEA.

NAEd (National Academy of Education). 2009. Standards, Assessments, and Accountability. Education Policy White Paper. Available online at *http://www.naeducation.org/Standards_ Assessments_Accountability_White_Paper.pdf.* (January 27, 2010)

NCES (National Center for Education Statistics). 2008. Digest of Education Statistics. Table 64, Public and private elementary and secondary teachers, enrollment, and pupil/teacher ratios: Selected years, fall 1955 through fall 2017. Available online at *http://nces.ed.gov/ programs/digest/d08/tables/dt08_064.asp.* (December 30, 2009)

NRC (National Research Council). 2002. Understanding the Influence of Standards: A Framework for Research in Mathematics, Science, and Technology Education. Washington, DC: National Academy Press.

Porter, A., M. Polikoff, and J. Smithson. 2008. Is There a De Facto National Curriculum: Evidence from State Content Standards? Paper presented at the workshop on Assessing the Role of K–12 Academic Standards in States, National Research Council Center for Education, January 18, 2008, Washington, D.C. Available online at *http://www7. nationalacademies.org/cfe/Porter_Smithson%20State%20Standards%20Paper_Tables.pdf.* (January 22, 2010)

Rothman, R. 2003. Imperfect Matches: The Alignment of Standards and Tests. Commissioned paper prepared for the National Research Council Committee on Test Design for K–12 Science Achievement. Available online at *http://www7.nationalacademies.org/bota/Align-ment%20of%20Standards.doc.* (January 27, 2010)

Spillane, J. 2004. Standards Deviation. Cambridge, MA: Harvard University Press.

Weiss, I.R., J.D. Pasley, S. Smith, E.R. Banilower, and D.J. Heck. 2003. A Study of K–12 Mathematics and Science Education in the United States. Available online at *http://www.horizon-research.com/insidetheclassroom/reports/highlights/highlights.pdf.* (February 3, 2010)

3

Leveraging Existing Standards to Improve K–12 Engineering Education

In Chapter 2, the committee concluded that, although it is theoretically feasible to develop content standards for K–12 engineering education, there would be little value in doing so at this time. In this chapter, the committee describes two ways that standards in other subjects can be leveraged to boost the presence and improve the quality and consistency of K–12 engineering education in the United States. These complementary approaches, "infusion" and "mapping," involve working with existing educational standards at the national and state levels. If used widely and successfully, these complementary approaches could set the stage for a reconsideration of the need for traditional standards for K–12 engineering, but they have value even if such standards are never developed. For infusion and mapping to have the most impact, there must first be a consensus on the core ideas in engineering. Fortunately, although formal agreement on the most important ideas has not yet been achieved, the groundwork for it has been laid (Box 3-1).[1]

The Infusion Approach

In the context of standards and this report, infusion means including the learning goals of one discipline—in this case engineering—in educational standards for another discipline. Infusion would take advantage of times when standards were being revised to reinforce or articulate connections between ideas in the standards and engineering. Successful infusion would mean: (1) engineering content would be more prominent in standards for science, technology, and mathematics; (2) the relationship between engineering and other STEM disciplines would be clearer; and (3) engineering would be included in student assessments based on the standards.

Existing national and state standards documents present logical opportunities to infuse engineering learning goals. Thus they provide a basis for including engineering in curricula, instruction, assessment, and professional development, which will help establish engineering as a legitimate subject in K–12 education. This does not mean that school systems would suddenly require engineering for graduation or that there would be a widespread demand for engineering courses and stand-alone engineering standards. However, infusion would be a step toward putting engineering on a par with other school subjects in the eyes of students, educators, and the

---

[1] For additional discussion of core ideas, see Chapter 4.

public. It would also put engineering in a position to become more of a partner in improving teaching and learning in science, technology, and mathematics.

BOX 3-1
Core Engineering Concepts, Skills, and Dispositions in K–12 Education

The committee reviewed eight papers that attempt to identify core concepts, skills, and dispositions appropriate to K–12 engineering education (see annex to this chapter.) Most of these documents provided analyses of existing reports, articles, and other materials, and more than half also included opinions solicited from experts, mostly engineers and engineering educators. Although no two authors or research groups used exactly the same methodology or examined exactly the same source materials, all eight papers identified doing or understanding **design**—or both—as a "big idea" in engineering. This was the only concept or skill recognized by all.

In four of the papers, **systems** were identified as important, either as a concept or as a skill or disposition (i.e., "systems thinking"), and four identified **constraints** as a core concept. Four or more identified as important **optimization**, **modeling**, and **analysis**, which are both concepts and practices in engineering design. **Communication** was judged to be a critical skill in five papers, the same number that identified understanding the **relationship between engineering and society** as important. **Making connections between engineering and science, technology, and mathematics**, although a rather general idea that does not fit neatly into any of the three categories, emerged as highly relevant in six of the eight papers.

National Standards

Science Education Standards. At the national level, the infusion approach is evident in several existing STEM standards (e.g., Sneider and Rosen, 2009; see also Appendix B). For example, *National Science Education Standards* (*NSES*) emphasizes the interdependence of science and technology and suggests that students should understand and acquire the capabilities of engaging in technological design (NRC, 1996). In fact, engineering appears in numerous instances in *NSES* (Box 3-2). Although these do not add up to a comprehensive portrayal of the role of engineering in scientific activities, they do suggest an acknowledgment of the importance of engineering.

Although the other set of national science standards, *Benchmarks for Science Literacy* (AAAS, 1993), is predicated on a "scientific enterprise" of which mathematics, engineering, and technology are critical components, engineering is rarely mentioned. However, in *Science for All Americans* (*SFAA; AAAS, 1989*), which makes a case for scientific literacy and was the foundation for *Benchmarks*, considerable attention is paid to engineering, especially in the discussion on the nature of technology. Since *Benchmarks* is presented as an online publication (*http://www.project2061.org/publications/bsl/online*), it might be possible to transpose the *SFAA* engineering properties into graded benchmark statements and insert them appropriately. Engineering learning goals could also be inserted elsewhere in *Benchmarks*—particularly in the chapter on the designed world.

The NRC has initiated a new project to develop a framework for the next generation of K–12 science education standards (Robelen, 2010). Because one of four project "design teams" is charged with elucidating the big ideas in engineering and technology, the framework will almost certainly encourage learning goals related to engineering education. The new framework is expected to inform the development of new science standards by Achieve, Inc. (*www.achieve. org*), which has worked with ACT and The College Board in developing common core standards for English language arts and mathematics (Box 3-3).

BOX 3-2
Selected Engineering-Related Concepts, Skills, and Dispositions
in the National Science Education Standards

Students should make proposals to build something or get something to work better; they should be able to describe and communicate their ideas. Students should recognize that designing a solution might have constraints, such as cost, materials, time, space, or safety. (Grades K–4, p. 137)

Children should develop abilities to work individually and collaboratively and to use suitable tools, techniques, and quantitative measurements when appropriate. Students should demonstrate the ability to balance simple constraints in problem solving. (Grades K–4, p. 137)

Scientific inquiry and technological design have similarities and differences. Scientists propose explanations for questions about the natural world, and engineers propose solutions relating to human problems, needs, and aspirations. (Grades 5–8, p. 166)

Perfectly designed solutions do not exist. All technological solutions have trade-offs, such as safety, cost, efficiency, and appearance. Engineers often build in back-up systems to provide safety. (Grades 5–8, p. 166)

Students should demonstrate thoughtful planning for a piece of technology or technique. Students should be introduced to the roles of models and simulations in these processes (Grades 9–12, p. 192)

The daily work of science and engineering results in incremental advances in our understanding of the world and our ability to meet human needs and aspirations. (Grades 9–12, p. 203)

SOURCE: NRC, 1996.

BOX 3-3
K–12 Engineering Education and the Common Core

The goal of the common core initiative, coordinated by the National Governors Association and the Council of Chief State School Officers, is to increase the rigor and narrow the content of standards for core subjects in grades K–12, as well as to encourage consistent implementation of standards among the states. Although the vast majority of states have indicated a willingness to consider adopting the core standards, the fate of the initiative is still uncertain. Attempts to set common performance measures for student achievement could reveal dramatic differences that have been largely obscured until now by variations among state student assessments.

Participating states will be allowed to add as much as 15 percent more content of their choosing to the common standards. This could be an opening for engineering, especially if science is the next subject taken up in the common core process. However, one goal of the common core effort is to restrict the number of student learning goals, which could limit how much engineering content can be added. Even if common core science education standards are not forthcoming, the NRC framework for a new generation of science education standards is expected to include engineering content.

Interestingly, one of the states that have indicated they may not participate in the common core initiative is Massachusetts, a leader in K–12 engineering education.

Technology Education Standards. *Standards for Technological Literacy: Content for the Study of Technology* (*STL*; ITEA, 2000) has the most engineering content of the national STEM education standards. Three of the 20 *STL* standards are explicitly focused on engineering-related ideas and skills (Box 3-4), reflecting the close relationship between technology and engineering. Even *STL*, however, could increase the infusion of engineering, for example by adding engineering in Standard 3 ("The relationships among technologies and the connections between technology and other fields") and Standard 4 ("The cultural, social, economic, and political effects of technology"). This might mean rewording to emphasize the engineering connection rather than adding new content.

Reducing, or at least not increasing, the number of student learning goals would be important for *STL* standards, as it would be for the *Benchmarks* standards. A change in the emphasis on engineering in *STL* could most easily and logically be made if and when the standards, now 10 years old, are revised. The timing for such a revision seems advantageous in light of the recent vote by members of the International Technology Education Association to change the name of the organization to the International Technology and Engineering Educators Association (ITEEA, 2010).

BOX 3-4
Technological Literacy Standards with
an Explicit Focus on Engineering

Standard 8: Students will develop an understanding of the attributes of design.

Standard 9: Students will develop an understanding of engineering design.

Standard 11: Students will develop the abilities to apply the design process.

SOURCE: ITEA, 2000.

Mathematics Education Standards. In contrast to science and technology standards documents, which define technology in very broad terms, mathematics standards have tended to define technology more narrowly (i.e., as electronic tools) and do not refer to engineering at all, except as one of many fields in which mathematics is used (NCTM, 1989, 2000). Nevertheless, connections to engineering are implied in NCTM standards related to (1) problem solving and (2) making connections to subjects outside the mathematics curriculum.

For a long time, the mathematics education community has sought to embed the learning of mathematics in actual or concrete problems. The infusion of engineering-related ideas could be one way to accomplish that goal. However, the recently released common core state standards for mathematics do not even contain the word engineer or engineering (CCSSO and NGA, 2010).

Other Subjects. Engineering is relevant to many other subjects for which national K–12 content standards have been developed, and infusion could be attempted in these cases as well. The committee did not have the time or resources to examine in depth the standards for geography, social studies, history, civics, and the arts, but each of these provides potential opportunities for including engineering-related materials.

National Assessments. Infusion of engineering-related concepts is also occurring in national assessments, which are based largely on current standards documents. For example, the 2009 science assessment framework of the National Assessment of Education Progress (NAEP) requires that 10 percent of test items be devoted to assessing students' understanding of technological design, which is defined as a "science practice" (WestEd, 2007). A planned assessment of "technology and engineering literacy" being developed by the National Assessment Governing Board places significant emphasis on students' knowledge of the engineering design process (WestEd, 2010).

NAEP results, which are based on national sampling techniques, are important tools for tracking trends in student achievement and are used as benchmarks against certain international assessments. However, because NAEP assessments are considered to be "low stakes," that is, there are no meaningful consequences tied to good or poor performance, they have had minimal influence on teachers' instructional practices or students' motivation (Wise and DeMars, 2003).

State Standards

Currently, standards at the state level vary widely. Infusion thus will depend on the status of engineering education, the standards already adopted, openness to considering engineering as a significant K–12 discipline, and the level of involvement of postsecondary engineering faculty in K–12 education. Historically, as was noted in Chapter 2, the implementation of national content standards begins when states adapt them for their own purposes. Although both sets of national science education standards and the technological literacy standards are infused to varying degrees with engineering concepts—and more infusion is possible—the question is to what extent these concepts appear—or might appear in the future—at the state level. The possible emergence of common core science standards raises new possibilities, as well as constraints, for the inclusion of engineering learning goals.

A few states, including Massachusetts, Minnesota, New York, Oregon, Pennsylvania, Rhode Island, Tennessee, Vermont, and Washington, already include engineering learning goals, often in combination with technology concepts, in their science education standards[2] (Jacob Foster, Massachusetts Department of Education, personal communication, 2/3/10).[3] Infusion at the state level can take numerous forms. In Minnesota, Nature of Science and Engineering, one of four science-content strands, is meant to be embedded and used in the other three: Physical Sciences, Earth and Space Sciences, and Life Sciences (MDE, 2010). In Washington State, engineering ideas related to systems and problem solving are included as cross-cutting "essential academic learning requirements" (State of Washington OSPI, 2009)). In New York, science standards related to Analysis, Inquiry, and Design include learning goals related to engineering design (NYSDE, 1996a), and standards related to Interconnectedness: Common Themes, address a

---

[2] Although the committee considers it unlikely, one or more state standards for mathematics may include engineering-related content. However, because of budgetary and time constraints, the committee was unable to investigate this possibility.

[3] Koehler et al. (2006) mapped concepts from their own framework (Koehler et al., 2005) for high school engineering education to state science standards and found some alignment in nearly every state, with higher correspondence in states in New England and the Mid-Atlantic region. The researchers' alignment methodology relied on a very broad definition of engineering, however, and it is not clear that all of the instances of engineering in science standards would be classified that way by others.

number of key engineering ideas, such as systems thinking, models, and optimization (NYSDE, 1996b). Engineering design is also addressed in the New York standards for technology education.

Tennessee K–12 science standards include "embedded technology and engineering standards" alongside science standards at each K–12 grade band (TDE, 2009). Design and Technology, one of seven sections in Vermont's science, mathematics, and technology standards, includes standards related to technological systems, outputs and impacts, and designing solutions (State of Vermont DOE, 2000).

Massachusetts' Standards for Science and Technology/Engineering includes a separate set of "engineering/technology" standards (MDOE, 2006). The state also has an assessment in place that includes engineering-related items. One way to satisfy the science requirements for graduation in Massachusetts is to pass the technology/engineering assessment. However, very few students at the high school level have opted to take the test. In 2009, just 2 percent of ninth graders and 1 percent of tenth graders did so (MDESE, 2009). Most students chose to satisfy this requirement by taking an assessment in either biology or physics.

The 10-year process that led to the inclusion of engineering in the Massachusetts K–12 standards highlights some of the challenges to the infusion approach. For example, three of the key stakeholder groups—science educators, technology educators, and the engineering community— often disagreed about where engineering belonged in the curriculum.[4] Foster (2009) noted that this disagreement affected how readily technology/engineering was accepted as an element in the science curriculum.

The state has added licensure processes for new technology/engineering teachers, but very few are being trained. The fact that the existing pool of technology educators was grandfathered into the new system has caused confusion about who is actually qualified to teach engineering. A remaining problem, according to Foster, is that technology/engineering coursework is not counted as science credit for the purposes of college admission by the Massachusetts Department of Higher Education or by the National Collegiate Athletic Association for the purposes of scholarship eligibility. These examples illustrate some of the difficult issues involved in standards implementation.

The Mapping Approach

In this report, "mapping" is understood as drawing attention explicitly to how and "where" core ideas from one discipline relate to the content of existing standards in another discipline. Unlike infusion, which is a proactive effort to embed relevant learning goals from one discipline into standards for another, mapping is a retrospective activity to (1) draw attention to connections that may or may not have been understood by the developers of the standards; (2) increase the likelihood that educators will use engineering contexts as vehicles for making other subjects, such as science, more engaging; and (3) suggest that engineering materials might be used as a basis for developing curricula or teacher professional development programs. One limitation of mapping is that some important engineering concepts or skills may not map to existing standards.

---

[4] A similar debate occurred recently in New Jersey with a different result. In June 2009, the New Jersey Board of Education elected to add engineering learning goals to revised standards for technology education rather than to science standards, although the latter was seriously considered by state officials (McGrath, 2009).

Examples of Standards Mapping

Mapping has been used in other disciplines with some success. For instance, the ocean science community launched a mapping effort in 2004 that culminated, in 2007, with the identification of seven "essential principles" and 44 "fundamental concepts," which were then mapped to *NSES* (NRC, 1996). The mapping has been illustrated as a matrix in a brochure suitable for classroom use or as a resource for curriculum development (NGS, 2007). Since 2007, an informal network of ocean literacy organizations has continued to refine this approach and recently released a set of "conceptual flow diagrams" linking the ocean literacy principles to specific learning goals in four K–12 grade bands (see *http://www.coexploration.org/ocean literacy/usa/ocean_science_literacy/scope_and_sequence/home.html*). The diagrams resemble the concept mapping in the two-volume AAAS *Atlas of Science Literacy* (2001, 2007).

The ocean literacy mapping exercise has contributed to the establishment of grant programs at the National Science Foundation and the National Oceanic and Atmospheric Agency (NOAA), has influenced the development of new K–12 and postsecondary instructional materials, has been incorporated by several states into revisions of K–12 science standards, and has influenced programming at informal science education institutions (NMEA, 2009; Strang, 2008).

The U.S. Global Change Research Program (USGCRP, 2009), in concert with more than two dozen partner organizations, mapped ideas in climate literacy to both *NSES* and the *Benchmarks to Science Literacy* (AAAS, 1993). These efforts were influential in grant decisions by federal agencies, and several states have indicated that they intend to use the mapping in revisions of their science standards (Frank Niepold, NOAA, personal communication, February 2, 2010). Similar mapping exercises have been conducted in neuroscience (SFN, 2008), Earth science (*www.earthscienceliteracy.org*), and atmospheric science (*http://eo.ucar.edu/asl/pdfs/ASLbro-chureFINAL.pdf*).

As an alternative to adding environmental science to the curriculum, the *Resources for Environmental Literacy* series (NSTA, 2007) uses environmental "essential questions" to foster specific learning goals from *NSES* and *Benchmarks*. It was developed by the Environmental Literacy Council and the National Science Teachers Association.

Mapping Engineering to Other Standards

In theory, engineering concepts, skills, and dispositions could be mapped not only to standards in the closely related STEM subjects of science, mathematics, and technology, but also to standards in other subjects, such as history, civics, and art, in which advances in technology and engineering have been important factors. As attention increases on the importance of K–12 education in preparing young people for jobs and postsecondary education, engineering-related links to readiness standards for the workforce and college provide another opportunity for mapping.

In career technical education, for example, the State Career Clusters Initiative (*www.career clusters.org)* promotes knowledge and skill statements in 16 areas, including STEM subjects, as well as architecture and construction; arts, audio/video technology, and communication; information technology; and manufacturing. A 2007 survey revealed that 23 of 46 states were at a "mid-level stage" of implementing programs of study consistent with the career clusters framework (NASDCTEc, 2007).

The goal of the American Diploma Project (ADP; *www.achieve.org/ADPNetwork*) by Achieve, Inc. is to promote college readiness through the adoption by states of ADP benchmarks in English and mathematics. Four cross-disciplinary proficiencies are embedded in the benchmarks, all of which are potentially relevant to engineering: research and evidence gathering; critical thinking and decision making; communications and teamwork; and media and technology. The Partnership for 21st Century Skills has developed an outcomes-based framework (P21, 2009) that suggests the skills, knowledge, and expertise students will need to succeed in the workplace and in their lives outside of work. Among the recommended skills are creativity and innovation, critical thinking and problem solving, and communication and collaboration, traits consistent with engineering habits of mind proposed by the Committee on K–12 Engineering Education (NAE and NRC, 2009).

Mapping at the State Level

Because of the strong influence of state standards on what happens in classrooms and on teacher preparation in public institutions of higher education, a mapping strategy at the state level might be very effective. However, given the number and variability of standards from state to state, mapping efforts will have to overcome significant practical challenges.

For example, a core engineering idea that maps to the science standards in one state may or may not map to the standards in another state, and determining the alignment for 50 different states would be a major undertaking. (If common core science standards are adopted, the alignment problem would be less difficult, at least in theory.) Software has been developed by the Syracuse University Center for Natural Language Processing (*www.cnlp.org*) that can be used to find content matches between and among state standards. Teach Engineering (*www. teachengineering.org*), a project of the National Science Digital Library, is using this and related software to map the content of national and state science, technology, and mathematics standards[5] to its collection of more than 800 engineering-related curricular units, lessons, and activities.

Conclusion

This chapter describes infusion and mapping as complementary approaches that offer alternatives to the development of stand-alone content standards for K–12 engineering education. Engineering-related ideas have already been infused into some national and state standards, and more infusion will be possible as existing standards are revised. A few examples of standards mapping and some evidence of the efficacy of this approach suggest that mapping may be a viable tactic.

Both approaches could be impacted by what happens with common core standards, particularly if standards for science, which has provided more fertile ground for connecting to engineering than mathematics, are developed. The prospects for infusion and mapping will almost certainly improve if an agreement can be reached on the core concepts, skills, and

---

[5] The standards used in the analysis are in the collection of the Achievement Standards Network (*www.achievementstandards.org*),

dispositions of engineering at the K–12 level. Some progress has been made in this regard, but more will be necessary to achieve a meaningful consensus.

References

AAAS (American Association for the Advancement of Science). 1989. Science for All Americans: A Project 2061 Report on Literacy Goals in Science, Mathematics, and Technology. Washington, DC: AAAS.

AAAS. 1993. Benchmarks for Science Literacy. Project 2061. Washington, DC: AAAS.

AAAS. 2001. Atlas of Science Literacy, Volume 1. Project 2061. Washington, DC: AAAS.

AAAS. 2007. Atlas of Science Literacy, Volume 2. Project 2061. Washington, DC: AAAS.

ASEE CMC (American Society for Engineering Education Corporate Member Council). 2008. K–12 STEM Guidelines for All Americans. Available online at *http://www.asee.org/ activities/organizations/councils/cmc/upload/2009/CMC_K–12_STEM_Guidelines_for_all_ Americans.pdf.* (January 27, 2010)

CCSSO (Council of Chief State School Officers) and NGA (National Governors Association). 2010. Common Core State Standards for Mathematics. Available online at *http://www.core standards.org/assets/CCSSI_Math%20Standards.pdf.* (September 8, 2010)

Childress, V., and C. Rhodes. 2008 Engineering student outcomes for grades 9-12. The Technology Teacher 67(7): 5–12.

Childress, V., and M. Sanders. 2007. Core engineering concepts foundational for the study of technology in grades 6–12. Paper presented the National Symposium to Explore Effective Practices for the Professional Development of K–12 Engineering and Technology Education Teachers. Feb. 11–13, 2007. Dallas/Ft. Worth, Texas. Available online at *http://www. conferences.ilstu.edu/NSA/papers/ChildressSanders.pdf.* (January 27, 2010)

Custer, R.L., J.L. Daugherty, and J.P. Meyer. 2009. Formulating the conceptual base for secondary level engineering education—a review and synthesis. Paper presented at the NAE Workshop on Standards for K–12 Engineering, Washington, D.C., July 8–9, 2009. Available online at *http://www.nae.edu/Programs/TechLit1/K12stds/WorkshoponStandardsforK–12 EngineeringEducation/15095.aspx.* (January 27, 2010)

Foster, J. 2009. The Development of Technology/Engineering Concepts in Massachusetts Academic Standards. Paper presented at the NAE Workshop on Standards for K–12 Engineering, July 8–9, 2009, Washington, D.C. Available online at *http://www.nae.edu/ Programs/TechLit1/K12stds/WorkshoponStandardsforK–12EngineeringEducation/ 15163.aspx.* (February 4, 2010)

Hacker, M., M. DeVries, and A. Rossouw. 2009. CCETE Project: Concepts and Contexts in Engineering and Technology Education—Results of the International Research Study. Available online at *http://www.hofstra.edu/pdf/Academics/Colleges/SOEAHS/ctl/ CTL_Edu_Initiatives_CCETE_revised.pdf.* (March 12, 2010)

ITEA (International Technology Education Association). 2000. Standards for Technological Literacy: Content for the Study of Technology. Reston, VA: ITEA.

ITEEA (International Technology and Engineering Educators Association). 2010. ITEA Officially Becomes ITEEA. News release, March 1, 2010. Available online at *http://www.iteea.org/AboutITEEA/NameChange.pdf.* (April 30, 2010)

Koehler, C., E. Faraclas, S. Sanchez, S.K. Latif, and K. Kazerounian. 2005. Engineering Frameworks for a High School Setting: Guidelines for Technical Literacy for High School students. Proceedings of the 2005 American Society for Engineering Education Conference. Available online at *http://soa.asee.org/paper/conference/paper-view.cfm?id=21254*. (February 26, 2010)

Koehler, C., D. Giblin, D.M. Moss, E. Faraclas, and K. Kazerounian. 2006. Are Concepts of Technical & Engineering Literacy Included in State Curriculum Standards? A Regional Overview of the Nexus between Technical & Engineering Literacy and State Science Frameworks. Proceedings of the 2007 ASEE Annual Conference and Exposition. Available online at *http://soa.asee.org/paper/conference/paper-view.cfm?id=1712*. (February 5, 2010)

McGrath, E. 2009. K–12 engineering standards in NJ. Presentation to the NAE Workshop on Standards for K–12 Engineering, Washington, D.C., July 8–9, 2009

MDE (Minnesota Department of Education). 2010. Minnesota Academic Standards. Science K–12. 2009 Version. May 24, 2010. Available online at *http://education.state.mn.us/mdeprod/groups/Standards/documents/Publication/013906.pdf*. (September 2, 2010)

MDOE (Massachusetts Department of Education). 2006. Massachusetts Science and Technology/Engineering Curriculum Framework. October 2006. Available online at *http://www.doe.mass.edu/frameworks/scitech/1006.pdf*. (March 31, 2010)

MDESE (Massachusetts Department of Elementary and Secondary Education). 2009. Spring 2009 MCAS Tests: Summary of State Results. Table 30: 2009 statewide MCAS results: Classes of 2011 and 2012 number and percentage of students in grades 9 and 10 scoring Needs Improvement (NI) or higher in high school science and technology/engineering. Available online at *http://www.doe.mass.edu/mcas/2009/results/summary.pdf*. (February 4, 2010)

NAE and NRC (National Academy of Engineering and National Research Council). 2009. Engineering in K–12 Education: Understanding the Status and Improving the Prospects. Committee on K–12 Engineering Education. Washington, DC: National Academies Press.

NASDCTEc (National Association of Directors of Career and Technical Education Consortium). 2007. Career Clusters and Programs of Study: State of the States. April 2007. Available online at *http://www.careerclusters.org/resources/publications/State_of_the_States_Report.pdf*. (February 12, 2010)

NCTM (National Council of Teachers of Mathematics). 1989. Curriculum and Evaluation Standards for School Mathematics. Reston, VA: NCTM.

NCTM. 2000. Principles and standards for school mathematics. Reston, VA: NCTM.

NGS (National Geographic Society). 2007. Ocean Literacy. The Essential Principles of Ocean Sciences. K–12. An Ocean-Oriented Approach to Teaching Science Standards. Available online at *http://www.coexploration.org/oceanliteracy/documents/OceanLitChart.pdf*. (February 10, 2010)

NMEA (National Marine Educators Association). 2009. Special Report #3: The Ocean Literacy Campaign. Impacts of the Ocean Literacy Principles. December. Ocean Springs, MS: NMEA.

NRC (National Research Council). 1996. National Science Education Standards. Washington, DC: National Academy Press.

NSTA (National Science Teachers Association) Press. 2007. Resources for Environmental Literacy Series: Five Teaching Modules for Middle and High School Teachers. Arlington, VA: NSTA Press.

NYSDE (New York State Department of Education). 1996a. Learning Standards for Mathematics, Science, and Technology. Revised Edition, March 1996. Standard 1: Analysis,

Inquiry, and Design. Available online at *http://www.emsc.nysed.gov/ciai/mst/pub/mststa1_2.pdf.* (March 31, 2010)

NYSDE. 1996b. Learning Standards for Mathematics, Science, and Technology. Revised Edition, March 1996. Standard 6: Interconnectedness—Common Themes. Available online at *http://www.emsc.nysed.gov/ciai/mst/pub/mststa6_7.pdf.* (March 31, 2010)

P21 (Partnership for 21st Century Skills). 2009. P21 Framework Definitions. Available online at *http://www.21stcenturyskills.org/documents/P21_Framework_Definitions.pdf.* (February 12, 2010)

Robelen, E.W. 2010. Work begins on "next generation" of science standards. Education Week. February 10, 2010.

Sneider, C. 2006. Draft Learning Progressions for Engineering Design. Boston Museum of Science, November 12, 2006. Unpublished.

Sneider C., and L.P. Rosen. 2009. Towards a vision for engineering education in science and mathematics standards. Paper presented at the NAE Workshop on Standards for K–12 Engineering, Washington, D.C., July 8-9, 2009. Available online at *http://www.nae.edu/Programs/TechLit1/K12stds/WorkshoponStandardsforK–12EngineeringEducation/15091.aspx.* (February 2, 2010)

SFN (Society for Neuroscience). 2008. Neuroscience Core Concepts. The Essential Principles of Neuroscience. Available online at *http://downloads.climatescience.gov/Literacy/Climate%20Literacy%20Booklet%20Hi-Res.pdf.* (February 10, 2010)

State of Vermont DOE (Department of Education). 2000. Vermont's Framework of Standards and Learning Opportunities. Fall 2000. Updated 3/10/10. Available online at *http://education.vermont.gov/new/pdfdoc/pubs/framework.pdf.* (March 31, 2010)

State of Washington OSPI (Office of the Superintendent of Public Instruction). 2009. Washington State K–12 Science Learning Standards. June 2009. Available online at *http://www.k12.wa.us/Science/pubdocs/WAScienceStandards.pdf.* (March 31, 2010)

Strang. C. 2008. Education for ocean literacy and sustainability: Learning from elders, listening to youth. The Current: The Journal of Marine Education 24(3). Ocean Springs, MS: National Marine Educators Association.

TeachEngineering. 2009. Quality Review Rubric for Engineering Content. Available online at *http://www.teachengineering.org/documents/TE_Engr_reviewcriteriarubric_061008toNewReviewersCoBranded.pdf.* (February 14, 2010)

TDE (Tennessee Department of Education). 2009. Users Guide to the Tennessee Science Curriculum Framework. Available online at *http://www.state.tn.us/education/ci/sci/doc/Users_guide.pdf.* (March 31, 2010)

USGCRP (U.S. Global Change Research Program). 2009. Climate Literacy. The Essential Principles of Climate Science. A Guide for Individuals and Citizens. Available online at *http://downloads.climatescience.gov/Literacy/Climate%20Literacy%20Booklet%20Hi-Res.pdf.* (February 10, 2010)

WestEd. 2007. Science Assessment and Item Specifications for the 2009 National Assessment of Educational Progress. Science NAEP 2009. Available online at *http://www.nagb.org/publications/frameworks/naep2009-science-specs07.doc.* (February 5, 2010)

WestEd. 2010. Technology and Engineering Literacy Framework for the 2014 National Assessment of Educational Progress. Pre-publication Edition. Available online at *http://www.edgateway.net/cs/naepsci/download/lib/249/prepub_naep_tel_framework.pdf?x-r=pcfile_d.* (July 8, 2010)

Wise, S.L., and C.E. DeMars. 2003. Examinee motivation in low-stakes assessment: Problems and potential solutions. Paper presented at the annual meeting of the American Association of Higher Education Assessment Conference, Seattle, Washington, June 2003. Available online at *http://www.jmu.edu/assessment/wm_library/Examinee_Motivation.pdf.* (February 10, 2010)

ANNEX

Core Engineering Concepts, Skills, and Dispositions for K–12 Education, Various Sources

Source	Method	Design[1]	Cxs to STM	Eng & Society	Constraints	Communication[2]	System(s)	Systems thinking	Modeling	Optimization	Analysis	Collaboration/teamwork	Creativity	Knowledge of specific techs[3]	Nature of eng	Prototyping	Experimentation
Hacker et al. (2009)	International Delphi Study	✓		✓			✓		✓	✓							
Custer et al. (2009)	Literature review, focus groups, "reaction panel"	✓			✓		✓		✓	✓	✓			✓		✓	✓
NAE and NRC,[4] 2009	Consensus study	✓	✓			✓		✓	✓		✓	✓					
ASEE CMC (2008)	Meetings of experts	✓	✓	✓		✓							✓		✓		
Childress and Sanders (2007)	Literature review	✓	✓	✓	✓	✓						✓	✓				
Childress and Rhodes[5] (2008)	Focus groups and modified Delphi study	✓	✓		✓	✓			✓	✓	✓		✓				✓
Sneider (2006)	Literature review, experience with curriculum development	✓	✓	✓	✓			✓				✓		✓	✓		
Koehler et al. (2005)	Not specified	✓	✓	✓	✓	✓				✓	✓			✓		✓	
Total		8	6	5	5	5	2	2	4	4	4	3	3	3	2	2	2

---

[1] Includes both understanding and doing design.

[2] Communication includes use of computer and computer-based tools.

[3] Includes one or more of the following categories of technology: information and communication, energy and power, transportation, food and medicine, construction.

[4] The core concepts, skills, and dispositions from the study were taken from the three principles outlined in NAE and NRC, 2009, Chapter 6.

[5] Participants in the Childress and Rhodes Delphi study achieved consensus on 43 "outcome items" for high school students hoping to purse engineering in college. Only those ranked 3.5 or higher (on a 5-point Likert scale) are included in the table.

Core Engineering Concepts, Skills, and Disposition for K–12 Education, Various Sources

Study	Method	Visualization	Use, manage, assess tech	Trade-offs	Ethics	Materials	Resource	Functionality	Specifications	Sustainability	Innovation	Efficiency	Understands eng as career option	Knowledge of contemp. issues	Planning & mngmt skills	Decision making	Leadership	Optimism
Hacker et al. (2009)	International Delphi Study			✓		✓	✓		✓	✓								
Custer et al. (2009)	Literature review, focus groups, "reaction panel"	✓		✓				✓			✓	✓						
NAE and NRC, 2009	Consensus study				✓													✓
ASEE CMC (2008)	Meetings of experts																	
Childress and Sanders (2007)	Literature review				✓									✓	✓	✓	✓	
Childress and Rhodes (2008)	Focus groups and modified Delphi study	✓	✓										✓					
Sneider (2006)	Literature review, experience with curriculum development		✓															
Koehler et al. (2005)	Not specified																	
Total		2	2	2	2	1	1	1	1	1	1	1	1	1	1	1	1	1

4

Conclusions and Recommendations

The committee believes that the evolving status of K–12 engineering education severely limits the potential value of developing traditional content standards. For this reason, we conclude that an initiative to develop such standards should not be undertaken at this time. Instead, several steps should be taken to increase the presence and improve quality and consistency of engineering education for K–12 students in the United States.

Step 1: Reach Consensus on Core Ideas in Engineering

To take full advantage of the infusion and mapping approaches discussed in Chapter 3 and to support curriculum development, teacher professional development, and assessment in K–12 engineering education, the committee concludes that it is necessary to first identify the most important concepts, skills, and habits of mind in engineering. As has been done in other fields, such as ocean science, we should articulate essential core ideas, rather than developing standards.

These core ideas, or big ideas, might be thought of as a first step toward the development of content standards, essential elements on which educational standards would need to be based. Core ideas, which are distillations of the essential nature of a field or practice, will necessarily be few in number. Content standards typically elaborate these core ideas as grade- or age-specific benchmarks or learning progressions based, when possible, on research in the cognitive sciences.

However, even if the core ideas do not lead to full-fledged standards, they will still be useful. They may, for example, prompt research that clarifies learning progressions for basic concepts, say, the idea of constraints. And their lack of specificity can provide flexibility for the various groups, from guidance counselors and teachers to test and textbook developers, interested in K–12 engineering education. Table 4-1 summarizes the key differences between content standards for K–12 engineering education and core ideas in engineering.

RECOMMENDATION 1. Federal agencies, foundations, and professional engineering societies with an interest in improving precollege engineering education should fund a consensus process to develop a document describing the core ideas—concepts, skills, and dispositions—of engineering that are appropriate for K–12 students. The process should incorporate feedback from a wide range of stakeholders. Work should begin as soon as possible, and the findings should be shared with key audiences, including developers of new or revised standards in science, mathematics, engineering, and technology at the national and state levels.

TABLE 4-1   Comparison of the Dimensions of Core Ideas and Standards in K–12 Engineering Education

Dimension	Standards	Core Ideas
Number of concepts, skills, dispositions specified	Similar to existing standards in science, mathematics, and technology	Many fewer
Time and funding to develop	Many years and several million dollars	Approximately one year and $1 million
Purpose	Blueprint for curriculum development, teacher professional development, and assessment	High-level statement of principles to inform groups interested in K–12 engineering education; general guidance for improving existing curriculum, teacher professional development, and assessment; basis for research on learning progressions
Level of specificity	Significant	Much more general
Conceptual coverage	Comprehensive and detailed	A subset of the most important "big ideas" with much less detail
Inclusion of grade bands or learning progressions	Yes	No

The committee further suggests that participant stakeholder groups in building a consensus on core ideas in engineering include the following:

- Science, technology, engineering, and mathematics professional societies
- Schools of engineering
- Engineering and technology education accreditation bodies
- Employers of engineers (e.g., technology-intensive industries)
- K–12 science, technology, engineering, and mathematics education associations
- The career technical-education community
- Organizations with a history and interest in development of K–12 education standards
- K–12 teacher accreditation bodies
- States that include or have attempted to include engineering in their K–12 standards
- Developers of K–12 student assessments
- Developers of K–12 curricula, instructional materials, and textbooks
- Organizations interested in college and workforce readiness

- Informal and after-school education organizations
- Parent-teacher organizations

Once a consensus has been reached, the core ideas will be useful in a variety of ways. First, they will provide a foundation and direction for the infusion and mapping approaches described in Chapter 3. The consistency and authority of both approaches will be reinforced by having agreed engineering ideas and practices to draw upon. One important use of the core ideas might be to inform the engineering portions of the expected new standards for K–12 science education to be developed by Achieve, Inc. in 2011. Another might be to strengthen the engineering content in the International Technology and Engineering Educators Association's *Standards for Technological Literacy*, if and when they undergo revision.

Second, the core ideas will be a resource for improving existing or creating new curricula, conducting teacher professional development, designing assessments, and informing education research.

Third, although the committee's focus was on questions related to the development and implementation of standards for the K–12 classroom, we recognize that there are also many opportunities for young people—and adults—to learn about engineering outside the formal school setting. Indeed, student involvement in out-of-school learning environments may equal in-class exposure for some subjects, such as science (Chi et al., 2008). Core ideas will provide guidance for people who work in informal education settings, such as museums, and after-school programs.

Part of the committee's charge was to consider how, or whether, standards for engineering education in K–12 would differ depending on whether the overall purpose is to support the goal of general literacy (the "mainline") or to target a narrower group of students who are interested in pursuing careers in engineering (the "pipeline"). The committee believes that the identification of core ideas in engineering will be beneficial for both purposes.

Ultimately, curriculum developers, providers of professional development, and others with an engineering-pipeline orientation may build on the foundation provided by core ideas by emphasizing connections between engineering and mathematics and science, especially physics. Educators with a mainline focus may use core ideas to develop resources for traditional science, mathematics, and technology education classes or informal or after-school programs.

Step 2: Provide Guidelines for the Development of Instructional Materials

The value of core ideas will be greatly enhanced for all purposes if they are embedded in "guidelines" for the development of instructional materials (cf., Rutherford, 2009). The purpose of the guidelines would be to improve the quality of engineering education materials, accelerate their development, and increase the number of individuals and groups that can use them, without developing actual standards.

Guidelines would necessarily include the core ideas in engineering, but they would also address other considerations, which we know from research and practice are important to ensuring the quality of instructional materials (Box 4-1). In other words, guidelines would not include all of the characteristics of effective educational curricula; they would include only the characteristics for which we have some basis in experience and understanding. The guidelines should be revised and improved as our knowledge grows and improves.

If supporters of improvements in K–12 STEM education (e.g., federal agencies, business and industry, foundations) champion these guidelines, they could have a rapid, positive effect on the development of K–12 engineering curricula that would be based on a more focused and more representative idea of the practice of engineering. Guidelines could provide a framework for assessment development in engineering as well as lay the groundwork for the possible development of content standards. If guidelines were incorporated into in-service and pre-service teacher education, prospective and current teachers would be prepared to create lesson plans that incorporate engineering principles. The same guidelines could be a useful resource for educators in informal education settings.

RECOMMENDATION 2. The U.S. Department of Education, National Science Foundation, Department of Energy, National Aeronautics and Space Administration, and other agencies with interest in engineering research and education should fund the development of guidelines for K–12 engineering instructional materials. Development should be overseen by an organization with expertise in K–12 education policy in concert with the engineering community. Other partners should include mathematics, science, technology education, social studies, and English-language-arts teacher professional societies; curriculum development and teacher professional development experts; and organizations representing informal and after-school education. Funding should be sufficient for an initial, intense development effort that lasts for one year or less, and additional support should be provided for periodic revisions as more research data become available about learning and teaching engineering on the K–12 level.

The committee suggests that the guidelines be made available online and periodically revised as data become available on the impact of engineering education on student learning in engineering as well as in science, mathematics, and technology; improvements in technological literacy; awareness and interest in engineering as a career option; and how students develop design ideas and practices over time.

Because guidelines would not have the same standing as standards, teachers, developers of instructional materials, and others may not follow them unless they are required to do so by funding agencies, state law, or local policy. In addition, if guidelines are, or are perceived to be, leading to a silo approach to K–12 engineering education, they could arouse resistance to the integration of engineering material and ideas into mathematics, science, and technology education.

Step 3: Boost Research on Learning

Developing consensus on core concepts, skills, and dispositions in K–12 engineering education and creating guidelines for the development of instructional materials will be important steps toward more consistent and higher quality K–12 engineering education. However, the committee believes that continuous improvement will require ongoing research to answer fundamental questions about how young people learn and understand engineering. This was an important point in the research-related recommendations in *Engineering in K–12 Education: Understanding the Status and Improving the Prospects* (NAE and NRC, 2009). We endorse those recommendations, urge that their relevance to the infusion and mapping approaches described in this report be considered, and suggest that they be expanded.

BOX 4-1
Possible Features of Guidelines for K–12 Engineering Instructional Materials

CORE ENGINEERING CONCEPTS, SKILLS, AND DISPOSITIONS
The guidelines should describe the essential content of engineering (e.g., systems, constraints, modeling, analysis, optimization, creativity, collaboration, communication, connection between engineering and society) and provide examples of how they play out in instructional materials

ELEMENTS OF ENGINEERING DESIGN
The guidelines should describe the elements of engineering design (e.g., problem identification, research, brainstorming of solutions, experimentation, prototyping) in a way that emphasizes that the process is nonlinear and that there is no single "correct" solution.

CONNECTIONS BETWEEN ENGINEERING AND OTHER SUBJECTS
The guidelines should describe how core ideas in engineering relate to other content areas. For example, engineering design and scientific inquiry share a number of features that make them useful problem-solving techniques. Inquiry can be used to develop data necessary to solving a design problem. Connections with mathematics include data collection and analysis, modeling, and estimation.

PEDAGOGY
The guidelines should elaborate how engineering design can be used as a pedagogical approach that encourages contextual, student-centered learning and provides meaningful opportunities for applying mathematical and scientific concepts.

FINDINGS FROM THE COGNITIVE SCIENCES
The guidelines should summarize some of the most significant findings from the cognitive sciences, both about learning in general and about learning engineering specifically. In engineering, for example, we know that engineering design activities must allow sufficient time for purposeful iteration and redesign for them to have an impact on conceptual learning,

DIVERSITY
The guidelines should emphasize the need for engineering education materials that appeal to diverse student populations, point out language and images that are known to discourage interest among these populations, and provide representative examples of instructional materials designed to appeal to students of all backgrounds.

EXAMPLES FROM EXISTING CURRICULA
The guidelines should include representative activities from existing elementary, middle, and high school engineering curricula.

RESOURCES AND IMPLEMENTATION
The guidelines should describe the need for various kinds of equipment needs and the costs associated with different models of engineering education, as well as some of the practical and policy issues related to implementation.

Recommendation 3. The following research questions should be part of a wide-ranging research agenda in K–12 engineering education funded by the National Science Foundation, other federal agencies, and the private sector:

- How do children come to understand (or misunderstand) core concepts and apply (or misapply) skills in engineering?
- What are the most effective ways of introducing and sequencing engineering concepts and skills for learners at the elementary, middle, and high school levels?
- What are the most important synergies in the learning and teaching of engineering and mathematics, science, technology, and other subjects?
- What are the most important considerations in designing materials, programs, assessments, and educator professional development that engage all learners, including those historically underrepresented in engineering?
- What are the best settings and strategies for enabling young people to understand engineering in schools, informal education institutions, and after-school programs?

Step 4: Measure the Impact of Reforms

The committee is aware how difficult it can be to measure the impact of reform efforts in K–12 education. Even when quality evaluations are conducted, it can be very hard to determine which educational interventions are most effective (e.g., DOEd, 2007). Despite these challenges, however, the committee concludes that in the case of standards infusion and mapping, core ideas, and guidelines for instructional materials development, it will be very important to assess how these efforts affect the development of K–12 engineering education in the United States over time. It will also be important to compare reforms in this country with efforts in other countries to introduce engineering to precollege students. Such data will provide a basis on which to either modify or discontinue one or more of these efforts.

Recommendation 4. Federal agencies with an interest in improving STEM education should support a large-scale survey to establish a comprehensive picture of K–12 engineering education nationally and at the state level. The survey should encompass formal and informal education, including after-school initiatives; build on data collected in the recent National Academies report on K–12 engineering education; and be conducted by an experienced education research organization. The survey should be periodically repeated to measure changes in the quality, scale, and impact of K–12 engineering education, and it should specifically take into account how the recommended practices of infusion and mapping, consensus on core ideas in engineering, and the development of guidelines for instructional materials have contributed to change. An effort should be made to compare the survey data with impact data from other countries' efforts to introduce engineering to precollege students.

The committee suggests that measurable "indicators," such as those proposed in Box 4-2, be developed to guide the research.

The survey data, combined with new findings from research on how K–12 engineering education is affecting student learning and interest in STEM disciplines, should be used to reassess the need for content standards for K–12 engineering education, modification of the

---

BOX 4-2
Suggested "Indicators" for Gauging the Impact of Infusion and Mapping,
Core Ideas, and Guidelines for the Development of Instructional Materials

Input indicators:

- state or national standards in science, mathematics, technology, or other subjects that include or connect to engineering concepts as described in the infusion and mapping approaches
- new or revised curricula in science, engineering, technology, mathematics, or other subjects that include engineering concepts as reflected in the core ideas in engineering or guidelines for the development of instructional materials
- school districts, institutions of higher education, curriculum projects, or other groups that provide teacher professional development consistent with the core ideas or guidelines
- K–12 teacher preparation programs that use or adopt the core ideas or appropriate features of the guidelines into their course offerings for prospective teachers
- informal and after-school education initiatives that offer students the opportunity to participate in engineering activities consistent with the core ideas and guidelines

Outcome indicators:

- student understanding of core ideas in engineering
- student achievement, interest, or motivation to learn mathematics, science, or technology that can be related to the introduction of engineering education consistent with the core ideas or guidelines
- schools, school districts, or states that adopt new or revised STEM curricula that include engineering concepts as reflected in the core ideas or guidelines
- K–12 teachers who can demonstrate understanding of core engineering ideas and how these ideas can be introduced to students

---

guidelines for instructional materials and the infusion and mapping approaches, and the creation of other kinds of resources for improving the quality and consistency of K–12 engineering education.

A Final Word

This study was conducted during a period of intense scrutiny of U.S. K–12 education. Concerns about the nation's innovation capacity, aggravated by the economic downturn that began in 2008, have directed attention to the importance of STEM subjects. Policy makers and others are concerned about data that seem to reflect poorly on U.S. student achievement in science and mathematics.

Historically, in elementary and secondary schools the "E" in STEM has been virtually silent. But a small and apparently growing number of efforts are now under way to introduce engineering experiences to K–12 students. Limited but intriguing evidence suggests that engineering education can not only improve students' understanding of engineering but also stimulate interest and improve learning in mathematics and science.

Currently there are no content standards, the traditional tool for guiding curriculum development, teacher education, and learning assessment, for engineering. Standards in other subjects have reshaped many key elements of the U.S. education system, but their impact on student learning appears to be limited. In addition, the implementation of standards varies from state to state, and concerns about this variability have led to a rapidly moving initiative to develop common core standards.

This is the environment in which the committee attempted to determine the need for content standards for K–12 engineering education. Although we conclude that such standards are not now warranted, this in no way diminishes our enthusiasm for the potential value of engineering education to our country's young people and, ultimately, to the nation as a whole. For a country like the United States, which is dependent on technological development, we can think of few subjects as critical as engineering to building an informed, literate citizenry, ensuring our quality of life, and addressing the serious challenges facing our country and the world.

References

Chi, B., J. Freeman, and S. Lee. 2008. Science in After-School Market Research Study: A Final Report to the S.D. Bechtel, Jr., Foundation. Coalition for Science after School and Center for Research, Evaluation and Assessment. Lawrence Hall of Science, University of California, Berkeley.

DOEd (U.S. Department of Education). 2007. Report of the Academic Competitiveness Council. Washington, DC: DOEd. Also available online at *http://www.ed.gov/about/inits/ ed/competitiveness/acc-mathscience/index.html*. (April 9, 2010)

NAE and NRC (National Academy of Engineering and National Research Council). 2009. Engineering in K–12 Education: Understanding the Status and Improving the Prospects. Committee on K–12 Engineering Education. Recommendations 1, 2, 3, 6, and 7. Washington, DC: National Academies Press.

Rutherford, J. 2009. Standards 2.0: New models for the new century: Alternatives to traditional content standards. Paper presented at the NAE Workshop on Standards for K–12 Engineering Education, Washington, D.C., July 8, 2009. Available online at *http://www.nae.edu/ File.aspx?id=15167*. (April 9, 2010)

ANNEX

General Principles for K–12 Engineering Education

Principle 1. K–12 engineering education should emphasize engineering design.

The design process, the engineering approach to identifying and solving problems, is (1) highly iterative; (2) open to the idea that a problem may have many possible solutions; (3) a meaningful context for learning scientific, mathematical, and technological concepts; and (4) a stimulus to systems thinking, modeling, and analysis. In all of these ways, engineering design is a potentially useful pedagogical strategy.

Principle 2. K–12 engineering education should incorporate important and developmentally appropriate mathematics, science, and technology knowledge and skills.

Certain science concepts as well as the use of scientific inquiry methods can support engineering design activities. Similarly, certain mathematical concepts and computational methods can support engineering design, especially in service of analysis and modeling. Technology and technology concepts can illustrate the outcomes of engineering design, provide opportunities for "reverse engineering" activities, and encourage the consideration of social, environmental, and other impacts of engineering design decisions. Testing and measurement technologies, such as thermometers and oscilloscopes; software for data acquisition and management; computational and visualization tools, such as graphing calculators and CAD/CAM (i.e., computer design) programs; and the Internet should be used, as appropriate, to support engineering design, particularly at the high school level.

Principle 3. K–12 engineering education should promote engineering habits of mind.

Engineering "habits of mind" align with what many believe are essential skills for citizens in the 21st century. These include (1) systems thinking, (2) creativity, (3) optimism, (4) collaboration, (5) communication, and (6) attention to ethical considerations. Systems thinking equips students to recognize essential interconnections in the technological world and to appreciate that systems may have unexpected effects that cannot be predicted from the behavior of individual subsystems.

Creativity is inherent in the engineering design process. Optimism reflects a world view in which possibilities and opportunities can be found in every challenge and an understanding that every technology can be improved. Engineering is a "team sport"; collaboration leverages the perspectives, knowledge, and capabilities of team members to address a design challenge. Communication is essential to effective collaboration, to understanding the particular wants and needs of a "customer," and to explaining and justifying the final design solution. Ethical considerations draw attention to the impacts of engineering on people and the environment; ethical considerations include possible unintended consequences of a technology, the potential disproportionate advantages or disadvantages of a technology for certain groups or individuals, and other issues.

Appendix A

Committee Biographies

Robert M. White (NAE), *chair*, is University Professor Emeritus of Electrical and Computer Engineering and Public Policy at Carnegie Mellon University (CMU) and consulting professor of Materials Science and Engineering at Stanford University. From 1993 to 1999, he was head of the Electrical and Computer Engineering Department and from 1999 to 2004 director of the Data Storage Systems Center at CMU. For his leadership as Under Secretary of Commerce for Technology under the first President Bush, he received the Public Service Award from IEEE. Prior to his government service, Dr. White spent six years at Control Data Corporation (CDC), where, as a member of the management board, he established and managed CDC's participation in the research consortium, Microelectronics and Computer Technology Corporation. In his early career, he was an assistant professor of physics at Stanford University and principal scientist at Xerox Corporation's Palo Alto Research Center for 13 years. The author of four books and many technical articles, Dr. White received his B.S. from MIT and his Ph.D. from Stanford (both in physics). Dr. White's most recent involvement at the National Academies was as chair of the Oversight Board for Capitalizing on Science, Technology, and Innovation: An Assessment of the Small Business Innovation Research Program.

Todd R. Allen, president and founder of Allen Research, Technologies and Services, Inc. (ARTS, Inc.), has worked in the health care industry with Johnson & Johnson (New Jersey) since 1994 as global manager of engineering, consumer products research, and development operations. Since 2003, he has established models and managed programs for assessing talents and leadership for scientists and engineers at the Ph.D., M.S., and B.S. levels and candidates for the international M.B.A. With more than 25 years of professional engineering practice in the petrochemical, nonwoven materials, and personal products industries and markets, he has also served on many committees in government, academia, and professional organizations, such as the National Science Foundation, American Society of Mechanical Engineers, American Association of Engineering Societies, American Association of Community Colleges, American Society for Engineering Education, and the National Urban League. A volunteer chef for the Philadelphia Helping Hand Rescue Mission and a licensed Christian minister, he champions diversity and inclusion as a strategy for national economic growth, national competitive advantage, and local community development. Mr. Allen received a B.S. in engineering from Georgia Tech, an M.S. in engineering from Tulane University, and an M.S. in engineering management from Syracuse University.

47

Christine Cunningham, vice president at the Museum of Science, Boston, and founder and director of the Engineering is Elementary (EiE) project, oversees the development of curricular materials, teacher professional development, and research and evaluation related to learning and teaching K-16 engineering and science. Her focus is on making engineering and science relevant, understandable, and accessible to everyone, especially marginalized populations, such as women, underrepresented minorities, and people with disabilities. The EiE project (*EiE, www.mos.org/eie*), founded in 2003, is creating a research-based, standards-based, classroom-tested curriculum that integrates engineering and technology concepts and skills with elementary science topics. As EiE director, Dr. Cunningham is responsible for setting the vision and strategy and securing funding (to date more than $22 million in grants) to support her projects and research. She earned a joint B.A. and M.A. in biology from Yale University and a Ph.D. in science education from Cornell University.

Heidi A. Diefes-Dux, an associate professor in the School of Engineering Education at Purdue University, received her B.S. and M.S. in food science from Cornell University and her Ph.D. in agricultural and biological engineering from Purdue University. As director of teacher professional development for the Institute for P-12 Engineering Research and Learning (INSPIRE), she has developed week-long summer academies and shorter programs for elementary school teachers interested in integrating engineering concepts into their instructional materials. Since 2006, more than 350 teachers in 17 states have attended the academies. Dr. Diefes-Dux is also principal investigator of "R&D: Quality Cyber-Enabled, Engineering Education Professional Development to Support Teacher Change and Student Achievement," a Discovery Research K–12 Project funded by the National Science Foundation. The purpose of the project is to develop a learning progression for elementary school teachers to improve their capability of adopting and refining engineering learning materials in the classroom. Dr. Diefes-Dix also conducts research on developing, implementing, and assessing authentic mathematical modeling problems for K–16 settings. She is a coauthor of *Models and Modeling in Engineering Education: Designing Experiences for All Students* (Sense Publishers, 2008).

Mario Godoy-Gonzales is the English as a Second Language/bilingual teacher of science, biology/biotechnology, mathematics, reading, writing, and world history at Royal High School in Royal City, Washington. After emigrating from Chile in 1994, he began his career teaching the children of migrant workers. In 1996, he participated in a summer professional development workshop at the Science Education Partnership at the Fred Hutchison Cancer Research Center, where he was introduced to the emerging field of biotechnology, which became the jumping-off point for his science classes. Later, a summer research fellowship from the M.J. Murdock Trust enabled him to conduct his own research at Central Washington University. Mario has received numerous awards, such as the Golden Apple for Excellence in Education in Washington State, Washington State Migrant Education Teacher of the Year, NEA/NFIE Donna Rhodes Award for Innovation in Education through the Use of Technology in the Classroom, National Science Teachers Association (NSTA) Gustav Ohaus Award for Innovation in Science Teaching, MIT Network of Educators in Science and Technology Outstanding Teacher of the Year, and Amgen Award for Science Teaching Excellence. He has given numerous presentations (e.g., to the Society for Advancement of Chicanos and Native Americans in Science [SACNAS] and NSTA) describing his experiences and has received many grants (e.g., the NSTA Toyota TAPESTRY grant and the NEA Innovation grant). Mario is also deeply involved with his community (coaching sports and leading the Cub Scouts) and is on the Washington State Hispanic Think Tank, Latino/ Latina Educational Achievement Project, and Teacher Advisory Council for the National Academy of Sciences, the SACNAS Pre-College Board, and the Washington State Student Biotech Expo. He has a B.A. from la Universidád de Chile and an M.A. in curriculum from la Universidád de Antofagasta, Chile.

Pam B. Newberry, director of strategic curriculum initiatives for Project Lead The Way (PLTW), coordinates and ensures the quality of new curricula and is the curriculum instructional designer for the PLTW Virtual Academy (an online resource for educators). From 2002 to 2004, she was PLTW associate director of curriculum, and from 2004 to 2007, she was director of curriculum. Prior to that, she was associate director of the International Technology Education Association (ITEA) Technology for All Americans Project, where she was involved in the development of the ITEA *Standards for Technological Literacy.* As a classroom teacher, Pam received the 1993 Presidential Award for Excellence in Mathematics and Science Teaching, was named 1994 Teacher of the Year for Mathematics for Virginia, and was designated a National Teacher Training Institute Master Teacher by the Corporation for Public Broadcasting and Texaco. In 1996, as an Albert Einstein Distinguished Educator Fellow, she spent eight months working in the Education Division at the National Aeronautics and Space Administration headquarters in Washington, D.C. She was also the recipient of the 2000–2001 Phi Delta Kappa Outstanding Educator Award. Ms. Newberry has a B. S. in industrial arts education (1975) and an M.A., an integrated degree in curriculum and instruction in technology/science/mathematics (1997), from Virginia Polytechnic Institute and State University.

Linda P. Rosen is CEO of Change the Equation, an initiative of corporate leaders who are connecting and aligning their efforts to transform science, technology, engineering, and mathematics K–12 learning in the United States. Previously, she was president of Education and Management Innovations, a consulting company focused on K–12 STEM education policy and teacher preparation professional development. She has also served as senior vice president for the National Alliance of Business; a senior adviser at the U.S. Department of Education; executive director of the National Commission on Mathematics and Science Teaching for the 21st Century (also known as the Glenn Commission); executive director of the National Council of Teachers of Mathematics (NCTM), where she launched the 2000 revision of the NCTM mathematics standards; and associate executive director of the Mathematical Sciences Education Board at the National Research Council. Dr. Rosen has taught mathematics and mathematics education courses for high school, college, and graduate students.

James Rutherford is retired education advisor to the Executive Officer of the American Association for the Advancement of Science (AAAS), where he was responsible for Science Resources for Schools, Challenge of the Unknown, the National Forum for School Science, Science Seminars for Teachers, and other national initiatives, as well as publications, including *Science Education News*, the annual science *Education Directory*, the annual *This Year in School Science*, and *Science Education in Global Perspective.* He initiated and directed Project 2061, a long-term, comprehensive effort to bring about nationwide reforms in science, mathematics, and technology education. Landmark publications from Project 2061 include *Science for All Americans, Benchmarks for Science Literacy, Blueprints for Reform, Resources for Science Literacy, Designs for Science Literacy,* and *Atlas of Science Literacy.* Prior to joining AAAS, in 1977 Dr.

Rutherford was appointed by President Carter to be assistant director of the National Science Foundation, where he was responsible for all science, mathematics, and engineering education programs and federal programs to improve the public understanding of science. When the new U.S. Department of Education was launched, Dr. Rutherford was appointed the first Assistant Secretary for Research and Improvement, where he oversaw the National Institute of Education, National Center for Educational Statistics, Fund for the Improvement of Post-Secondary Education, and federal programs supporting libraries and the development of educational technologies. Earlier in his career, Dr. Rutherford was a professor of science education at Harvard University and New York University, and earlier still, he was a high school science teacher in California. During his academic career, he directed several major projects, including Harvard Project Physics, Project City Science, and the Carnegie Science–Humanities Education Project. Dr. Rutherford was educated in the California public schools and earned degrees from the University of California, Berkeley, Stanford University, and Harvard University.

Christian D. Schunn is an associate professor of psychology and a research scientist at the Learning Research and Development Center at the University of Pittsburgh. His basic research involves studying experts and novices in complex domains like science, engineering, submarining, and weather forecasting to develop theoretical and computational models of the cognition underlying their performance and the difficulties in developing expert-like performance. He then conducts applied research to develop and evaluate tools and curricula informed by the results. Recently, his basic research has involved interdisciplinary collaboration with mechanical and industrial engineers on the nature of cognition underlying innovative engineering design processes, for example, the interaction between the physical design environment and analogical reasoning in highly innovative design groups. At the applied level, he has developed design-based learning curricula for middle and high school science classrooms that have been found to be more successful than existing hands-on and textbook science curricula at teaching basic science concepts and scientific reasoning skills and in stimulating interest in careers in engineering, science, and technology. Dr. Schunn received his Ph.D. from Carnegie Mellon University in 1995.

Susan Sclafani, director of State Services for the National Center on Education and the Economy (NCEE), works with a coalition of states committed to following the recommendations in *Tough Choices or Tough Times* (NCEE, 2007), beginning with the implementation of the Board Examinations System in high schools. From 2005 through 2008, as managing director of Chartwell Education Group, LLC, Dr. Sclafani worked with governmental and nonprofit organizations on education projects in the United States, India, the Middle East, and China. She also led international benchmarking visits for states and school districts to learn from the best practices of high-performing nations. As Assistant Secretary of Education for Vocational and Adult Education and Counselor to the Secretary of Education from 2001 to 2005, Dr. Sclafani was the U.S. representative to the Organisation for Economic Co-operation and Development and Asia-Pacific Economic Cooperation. While at the Department of Education, she created the Mathematics and Science Initiative, the High School Redesign Initiative, and the E-Language Learning Project with the Chinese Ministry of Education. Prior to serving in government, Dr. Sclafani held a variety of leadership positions, including chief of staff for Education Services for the Houston Independent School District. From 1975 to 1983, she helped start, and then led, the High School for Engineering Professions, a magnet school in Houston.

James ("Jim") C. Spohrer, director of IBM University Programs (IBM UP) since 2009, founded IBM's first Service Research Group in 2003 at the Almaden Research Center with a focus on STEM (science, technology, engineering, and mathematics) for Service Sector Innovations. Under his leadership, this group earned ten times its investment and received four IBM Outstanding and 11 Accomplishment Awards in seven years. Working with service research pioneers from many academic disciplines, Jim advocates for Service Science, Management, Engineering, and Design, an integrative extended-STEM framework for the development of global competency, economic growth, and the advancement of science. In 2000, he became the founding chief technical officer of IBM's first Venture Capital Relations Group in Silicon Valley. In the mid-1990s, he led Apple Computer's Learning Technologies Group, where he was named Distinguished Engineer Scientist and Technologist. Dr. Spohrer earned a Ph.D. in computer science/artificial intelligence from Yale University and a B.S. in physics from Massachusetts Institute of Technology.

Elizabeth K. Stage is director of Lawrence Hall of Science, the public science center at University of California, Berkeley. Previously, she was director of the Mathematics Professional Development Institutes under the Office of the President of the University of California. Dr. Stage has worked to increase opportunities for all students to learn mathematics and science. Her national service includes director of critique and consensus at the National Research Council (NRC) National Committee on Science Education Standards and Assessment. She is an elected fellow of the American Association for the Advancement of Science and a former member and chair of the California Curriculum Commission. She is also a member of the Science Standing Committee for the National Assessment of Educational Progress. In 1996, Dr. Stage was awarded the Smith College Medal. She has an Ed.D. in science education and an M.Ed., both from Harvard University, and an A.B. in chemistry from Smith College. She has been a member of the NRC Committee on the Review on Understanding the Influence of Standards in K–12 Science, Mathematics, and Technology Education (1998 to 2001) and the Committee on the Review and Evaluation of NASA's Pre-College Education Program (2006 to 2008).

Roberta Tanner teaches physics and other mathematics and science classes at Loveland High School in Loveland, Colorado, and has taught in the Thompson School District for 18 years. With help from a local engineer, she developed, and now teaches, a project-oriented course on microchips and electrical engineering for high school students. She also started the Advanced Placement physics program in her district. Ms. Tanner was teacher-in-residence with the Physics Education Research Group at the University of Colorado in 2006–2007 and received the Intel International Excellence in Teaching Award in 2004. She is currently a member of the National Academies Teacher Advisory Council. Ms. Tanner completed her undergraduate work in physics and mechanical engineering at Kalamazoo College and Michigan State University and earned her teaching certificate and a master's degree in education at the University of Colorado, Boulder. Before becoming a teacher, she worked as a mechanical engineer in product development at IBM.

Appendix B[1]

Commissioned Papers

[1] The commissioned papers have been lightly edited to remove spelling and other typographical errors but are otherwise the authors' original work.

K–12 ENGINEERING EDUCATION STANDARDS: OPPORTUNITIES AND BARRIERS

A Presentation for the
Workshop on Standards for K–12 Engineering Education

National Academy of Engineering
Keck Center of the National Academies

Rodger W. Bybee
Executive Director (Emeritus)
Biological Sciences Curriculum Study (BSCS)

8 July 2009
Washington, DC

STANDARDS FOR K–12 ENGINEERING EDUCATION: OPPORTUNITIES AND BARRIERS

Rodger W. Bybee

Introduction

Does the nation need standards for K–12 engineering education? The answer to this question is paradoxically both simple and complex. It requires an examination of a rationale for such standards as well as of opportunities and barriers to developing and implementing them.

The Idea of Standards

A contemporary agreement among 46 states to join forces and create common academic standards in math and English language arts makes it clear that the idea of standards has an overwhelming appeal to policy makers. National standards also have an unimaginable complexity for the educators responsible for "implementing" them (Bybee and Ferrini-Mundy, 1997; DeBoer, 2006; NRC, 2002). The current understanding of standards derives from the original meaning of a standard as "a rallying point for an army" which evolved to an "exemplar of measure or weight" to a statement of "correctness or perfection" and finally to a "level of excellence."

The primary functions of an educational standard are to rally support, increase coherence, and measure attainment. All of these functions require political persuasion, psychometric precision, and practical applications. In the end, setting standards, such as those being considered for K–12 engineering education, will require securing the allegiance of a broad constituency, addressing programmatic concerns beyond policy (e.g., school programs and teaching practices), and implementing an assessment system that is manageable and understandable to educators and the public.

Standards for education are statements about purposes, priorities, and goals (Hiebert, 1999). In engineering education, standards would be value judgments about what our students should know and be able to do. Education standards should be developed through a complex process informed by societal expectations, past practices, research information, and visions of professionals in associated fields (e.g., engineering and education).

Before we go further, several terms should be clarified. In general, discussions of academic standards and current considerations of engineering education standards refer to CONTENT STANDARDS—learning outcomes described as knowledge and abilities in a subject area. For example, students should learn concepts, such as systems, optimization, and feedback;

they should develop abilities in engineering design and habits of mind. Content standards are different from other standards, such as performance standards, professional development standards, and teaching standards (see Table 1).

Table 1   Some Terms Used in Standards-Based Reform

CONTENT STANDARDS. A description of the knowledge and skills students are expected to learn by the end of their schooling in a certain subject. Content standards describe learning outcomes, but they are *not* instructional materials (i.e., lessons, classes, courses of study, or school programs).

CURRICULUM. The way content is delivered. Curriculum includes the structure, organization, balance, and presentation of content in the classroom.

PERFORMANCE STANDARDS. A description of the form and function of achievement that serves as evidence that students have learned, usually described in relation to content standards. Performance standards sometimes identify levels of achievement (e.g., basic, proficient, advanced) for content standards.

TEACHING STANDARDS. Descriptions of the educational experiences provided by teachers, textbooks, and technology. Teaching standards should indicate the quality of instruction for students and may emphasize unique features, such as design experiences in engineering and the use of integrated instructional sequences.

The History of the Idea of Education Standards

More than a century ago, the Committee of Ten, a working group of educators assembled to standardize the American high school curriculum, recommended college admissions requirements, including that students had some experience in a science laboratory. The committee's report influenced numerous programs and practices in the nation's schools (DeBoer, 1991; Sizer, 1964). One example is especially relevant to national standards. The report was the impetus for the development of the Harvard Descriptive List, a description of experiments in physics to be used as part of the admission requirements for the college. Students applying to Harvard would be required to complete 40 experiments and a written test about the experiments and principles of physics. The point is that the Harvard Descriptive List meets the definition of an educational standard, a combination of content and teaching standards.

Since the late 1800s, numerous policies, generally in the form of committee reports, have described what are now referred to as educational standards, including standards for science. Technology and engineering were almost never mentioned. However, in recent decades, technology has often been (incorrectly) referred to as applied science.

In the late 1980s, in the latter years of the "Sputnik era," a new stage of education emerged, which can be characterized as the "standards era." The likely origin of this era is the 1983 report of the National Commission on Excellence in Education, *A Nation at Risk*. Two recommendations from that report set the stage for the development of educational standards: (1) strengthening the content of the core curriculum; and (2) raising expectations by using measurable standards. The report described course requirements in five core subjects—English, mathematics, science, social studies, and computer science—for high school graduation. To state the obvious, neither technology nor engineering was among the core subjects.

In 1989, then President George H.W. Bush and a group of governors (including Bill Clinton) met in Charlottesville, Virginia, for an Education Summit, the outcomes of which included National Education Goals, which led directly led to initiatives for voluntary national standards in each core subject. In the same year, 1989, the National Council of Teachers of Mathematics published *Curriculum and Evaluation Standards for School Mathematics* (NCTM, 1989), and the American Association for the Advancement of Science published *Science for All Americans* (AAAS, 1989). Both publications provided leadership for standards-based reform. Still, as Paul DeHart Hurd argued, standards are fine, but they are not a reinvention (Hurd, 1999)

The basic idea of standards-based reform was to establish clear, coherent, and challenging content as learning outcomes for K–12 education. The assumption was that voluntary national standards would be used by state education departments and local jurisdictions to select educational programs, instructional practices, and assessments that would help students meet the standards. An additional assumption was that undergraduate teacher education and professional development for classroom teachers would also be aligned with the standards. The basic idea may sound reasonable, but in reality it did not work as envisioned. As a result of the many independent decisions about teacher preparation, textbooks, tests, and teaching, the proposed national standards had less influence than desired (NRC, 2002). This said, the standards for science (NRC, 1996) have had a positive influence on the educational system, especially on state standards and curriculum materials (DeBoer, 2006).

The Emergence of the Idea of K–12 Engineering Standards

Based on *Science for All Americans* (AAAS, 1989), in 1993 the AAAS published *Benchmarks for Scientific Literacy*, and in 1996 the National Research Council published *National Science Education Standards*. These three documents include recommendations and standards related to engineering and technology. For example, *Science for All Americans* set the stage for increased recognition of engineering education with discussions of "Engineering Combines Scientific Inquiry and Practical Values" and "The Essence of Engineering Is Design Under Constraint" (AAAS, 1989, pp. 40–41).

The International Technology Education Association (ITEA) published *Standards for Technological Literacy* in 2000. An important point about these standards is that they paid substantial attention to the idea of engineering design and underwent a thorough review and subsequent revision by the National Research Council with input and criticism from the National Academy of Engineering.

In the two decades since 1989, the idea of national standards for education has been widely recognized as important, if not essential, and is increasingly being accepted by most policy makers and educators.

Purposes of National Standards

Before turning to a specific discussion of K–12 engineering education standards, I present my reflections and opinions based on more than a decade of experience with the *National Science Education Standards* (NRC, 1996). My work on these standards began in 1992 as a member (and later chair) of the Content Working Group. In 1995, I became executive director of the Center for Science, Mathematics, and Engineering Education at the National Academies, where I worked on completing and disseminating the *Standards* until 1999, when I returned to working on the Biological Sciences Curriculum Study (BSCS). At BSCS we used the standards as the content and pedagogical foundation for curriculum materials and professional development. So my experiences with standards have included the perspectives on policy, program, and practice. For those interested, Angelo Collins has provided an excellent history of the national science education standards (Collins, 1995). Also worth noting is the October 1997 issue of *School Science and Mathematics*, a theme issue for which my colleague, Joan Ferrini-Mundy, and I served as guest editors.

First and foremost, the power of national standards is their potential capacity to change the fundamental components of the education system on a scale that will make a difference. Very few things have the capacity to change curriculum, instruction, assessment, and the professional education of teachers. National standards are on the short list of things that could initiate system-wide changes on a significant scale. To the degree that various agencies, organizations, institutions, and districts embrace national standards, they have the potential to increase coherence and unity among state frameworks, criteria for the adoption of instructional materials, state assessments, and other resources.

Early in my work, I realized that there were several ways standards might affect the system, for example, in the teaching of biological evolution. First, including content such as biological evolution in national standards would affect the content in state and local science education standards. A review by *Education Week* (9 November 2005) found that a majority of states (39) included some description of evolution in their science standards.

Second, national standards can promote feedback within education systems. Using the science education standards as a basis for the review by *Education Week* provided insights into which states did *not* mention evolution. The review also indicated the significant variations in the presentation of evolution, a major finding.

Here is an example of my third point, that standards can be used to define the limits of acceptable content. When Kansas recently planned to adopt state standards that would promote nonscientific alternatives to evolution and liberally borrowed from the *Standards* and National Science Teachers Association (NSTA) publications, both organizations denied Kansas the right to use any of their material in its new standards (*Science*, 4 November 2005).

Fourth, standards influence the entire educational system because they both are input and define output. To identify and define output, we ask, "What should all students know, value, and be able to do?" The history of education has primarily focused on inputs with the hope of improving outputs—especially student learning. For example, we change the length of school years, courses, textbooks, educational technologies, and teaching techniques. All such inputs are meant to enhance learning, but they have been inconsistent, not directed toward a common purpose, and centered on different aspects of the educational system. In other words, they have not been coherently focused on common outcomes. The lack of coherence is clear in many contemporary analyses of the relationships among curriculum instruction, assessment, and professional development.

Fifth, national standards are policies for all students. By their very nature, national standards embrace equity. In the decade since the release of the standards, many individuals have asked me if we really meant *all* students. The answer is—yes. Of course, there are always exceptions (e.g., severely developmentally disabled students) that prove the rule. But the *Standards* are explicit statements of equity. While developing the *Standards*, we clearly understood that many aspects of the education system would have to change to accommodate the changes they implied. For example, resources would have to be reallocated to increase the achievement level of the students most in need.

Have the *Standards* changed the fundamental components of the educational system and achieved equity? No. But you will notice that I indicated they had the *potential* to do so. I would also note that this nation has not achieved equal justice for all, but we hold this as an important goal, one that we do not plan to change because it has not yet been achieved.

A Rationale for National Standards in Engineering Education

The justification for developing standards for engineering education rests on a foundation that includes both societal and educational perspectives. I begin with the societal perspective by looking first at history, in particular the 20th century.

One stunning example supports the case for engineering education standards. In late 1999, the Newseum, a journalism museum then located in Virginia, conducted a survey of American historians and journalists to determine the top 100 news stories of the 20th century. As I read the list, I was surprised that of the top 100 headlines, more than 40 percent were directly related to engineering and technology. This ranking of news stories seems to justify increasing the emphasis on engineering education and technological literacy, because they reflect what the public reads, hears, and values.

The high percentage of engineering-related news events is rivaled only by political events, many of which also indirectly involved engineering. Table 2 lists the engineering-related events (modified to include only stories with a direct component of engineering or technology). Each selection in Table 2 meets one of these criteria: (1) the story clearly is *about* engineering/technology; (2) the story has clear *connections* to engineering/technology; or (3) the story forecasts a future application for engineering/technology. As an interesting aside, in completing this analysis, I realized that nearly *all* of the headlines had some connection to engineering/technology.

Although some might debate particular selections, it would be difficult to argue with the general conclusion that a significant percentage of *important events* in the 20th century were clearly and directly related to engineering/technology. In the early years of the 21st century, I see no reason to predict fewer of those stories, and I think it reasonable to suggest that there will be more. The justification for promoting engineering and technology education seems clear.

Table 2   Engineering/Technology-Related News Stories of the 20th Century*

Engineering/Technology Ranking	Top 100 Ranking	Year	Headline
1	1	1945	U.S. drops Atomic bombs on Hiroshima, Nagasaki: Japan surrenders to end World War II
2	2	1969	American astronaut Neil Armstrong becomes the first human to walk on the moon
3	3	1941	Japan bombs Pearl Harbor: U.S. enters World War II
4	4	1903	Wilbur and Orville Wright fly the first powered airplane
5	11	1928	Alexander Fleming discovers the first antibiotic, penicillin
6	12	1953	Structure of DNA discovered
7	17	1913	Henry Ford organizes the first major U.S. assembly line to produce Model T cars
8	18	1957	Soviets launch Sputnik, first space satellite: space race begins
9	20	1960	FDA approves birth control pill
10	21	1953	Dr. Jonas Salk's polio vaccine proven effective in University of Pittsburgh tests
11	25	1981	Deadly AIDS disease identified
12	28	1939	Television debuts in America at New York World's Fair
13	30	1927	Charles Lindbergh crosses the Atlantic in first solo flight
14	31	1977	First mass market personal computers launched
15	32	1989	World Wide Web revolutionizes the Internet
16	33	1948	Scientists at Bell Labs invent the transistor
17	35	1962	Cuban Missile Crisis threatens World War III
18	36	1912	"Unsinkable" Titanic, largest man-made structure, sinks
19	40	1909	First regular radio broadcasts begin in America
20	41	1918	Worldwide flu epidemic kills 20 million
21	42	1946	"ENIAC" becomes world's first computer
22	43	1941	Regular TV broadcasting begins in the United States
23	46	1909	Plastic invented: revolutionizes products, packaging
24	48	1945	Atomic bomb tested in New Mexico
25	51	1959	American scientists patent the computer chip
26	52	1901	Marconi transmits radio signal across the Atlantic
27	57	1962	Rachel Carson's *Silent Spring* stimulates environmental protection movement
28	60	1961	Yuri Gagarin becomes first man in space
29	61	1941	First jet airplane takes flight
30	64	1942	Manhattan Project begins secret work on atomic bomb: Fermi triggers first atomic chain reaction
31	66	1961	Alan Shepard becomes first American in space
32	70	1961	Communists build wall to divide East and West Berlin
33	75	1928	Joseph Stalin begins forced modernization of the Soviet Union; resulting famines claim 25 million
34	78	1900	Max Planck proposes quantum theory of energy
35	79	1997	Scientists clone sheep in Great Britain
36	80	1956	Congress passes interstate highway bill
37	81	1914	Panama Canal opens, linking the Atlantic and Pacific oceans
38	83	1986	The Space Shuttle *Challenger* explodes, killing crew
39	87	1958	China begins "Great Leap Forward" modernization program, estimated 20 million die in ensuing famine
40	90	1962	John Glenn becomes first American to orbit the Earth
41	92	1997	*Pathfinder* lands on Mars, sending back astonishing photos
42	95	1978	Louise Brown, first "test-tube baby," born healthy
43	96	1948	Soviets blockade West Berlin: Western allies respond with massive airlift
44	97	1975	Bill Gates and Paul Allen start Microsoft Corp. to develop software for Altair computer
45	98	1986	Chernobyl nuclear plant explosion kills more than 7,000

*Modified from "The Top 100 News Stories of the 20th Century" (1999 USA TODAY, a division of Gannett Co., Inc.)

To the historical justification, one can add contemporary challenges (see, e.g., the NAE Grand Challenges project, *www.engineeringchallenges.org*) that include the role of engineering and innovation in economic recovery, the efficient use of energy resources, the mitigation of risks from climate change, the creation of green jobs, the reduction in health care costs, an increase in healthy life styles, improving defense, and the development of new technologies for national security.

Turning to educational justifications for standards for K–12 engineering education, I would first note the need for a widely accepted national statement of the goals and purposes of engineering education. I realize that individual curricula have goals. We can, for example, cite the historical goal of technological literacy from the 1970s Engineering Concepts Curriculum Project. Contemporary engineering curricula have similar goals (NAE, 2009). Nevertheless, I still believe we need a "widely accepted national statement" of the goals, purposes, and policies of engineering education.

STEM is a popular acronym for science, technology, engineering, and mathematics education. We have national standards for science (NRC, 1996), technology (ITEA, 2000), and mathematics (NCTM, 2000), but not for engineering education. I rest my case.

Finally, we are in an era of standards-based reform. To be recognized and accepted in education today, a discipline or area of study needs a set of standards.

Opportunities for Developing Standards for Engineering Education

The opportunities for standards for engineering education can be summed up in a short phrase—the time is right. A convergence of conditions has created a climate conducive to the emergence of engineering as a viable component of K–12 education.

In a recent editorial in *Science*, John Holdren, President Obama's science and technology advisor, presents four practical challenges for the Obama administration: bringing science and technology more fully to bear on economic recovery; driving the energy-technology innovation we need to reduce energy imports and reduce climate-change risks; applying advances in biomedical science and information technology; and ensuring the nation's security with needed intelligence technologies (Holdren, 2009). One can argue that all four challenges have essential connections to, and reliance on, engineering.

In the same editorial, Holdren introduced what he calls "cross cutting foundations" for meeting the challenges. One of the foundations was "strengthening STEM education at every level, from precollege to postgraduate to lifelong learning." (Holdren, 2009, p. 567). Since the National Science Foundation (NSF) introduced the term STEM as an acronym for science, technology, engineering, and mathematics,[*] it has become widely used to refer to STEM education. But the truth is, the acronym usually refers to either science or mathematics, or both. It seldom refers to technology and almost never includes engineering. So, although the nation is concerned about STEM education, the T is only slightly visible and the E is invisible. A major opportunity for standards in engineering education is to make the E in STEM education visible.

Standards for K–12 engineering education would define the knowledge and abilities for the E in STEM education and clarify ambiguities in the use of the acronym. However, unless engineering education standards are developed with tact and care, they could perpetuate the politics and territorial disputes among the science, technology, engineering, and mathematics disciplines. Given the history of the sovereignty of educational territory, I suggest that standards

---

[*] NSF actually began using the acronym SMET and later changed to STEM.

and engineering education, with support from business and industry, could provide leadership by providing a contemporary vision of STEM (Sanders, 2009).

Another opportunity is implied in a current theme and the stated outcomes of education—the development of 21st century skills. The National Research Council has presented a summary of those skills (see Table 3). Based on this list, K–12 activities that center on engineering design could substantially contribute to students' development of these skills. In this case, this may be a three-for-one opportunity. Students have opportunities to: (1) develop 21st century skills; (2) make connections to other STEM subjects; and (3) learn about careers in engineering. Overall, experience with engineering design would probably raise the level of students' understanding of engineering and, by so doing, expand their interest and motivation, so that many of them may one day pursue careers in science, technology, engineering, or mathematics.

Table 3   Examples of 21st Century Skills*

Research indicates that individuals learn and apply broad 21st century skills within the context of specific bodies of knowledge (National Research Council, 2008a, 2000; Levy and Murnane, 2004). At work, development of these skills is intertwined with development of technical job content knowledge. Similarly, in science education, students may develop cognitive skills while engaged in study of specific science topics and concepts.

1. **Adaptability:** The ability and willingness to cope with uncertain, new, and rapidly-changing conditions on the job, including responding effectively to emergencies or crisis situations and learning new tasks, technologies, and procedures. Adaptability also includes handling work stress; adapting to different personalities, communication styles, and cultures; and physical adaptability to various indoor or outdoor work environments (Houston, 2007; Pulakos, Arad, Donovan, and Plamondon, 2000).

2. **Complex communications/social skills:** Skills in processing and interpreting both verbal and non-verbal information from others in order to respond appropriately. A skilled communicator is able to select key pieces of a complex idea to express in words, sounds, and images, in order to build shared understanding (Levy and Murnane, 2004). Skilled communicators negotiate positive outcomes with customers, subordinates, and superiors through social perceptiveness, persuasion, negotiation, instructing, and service orientation (Peterson et al, 1999).

3. **Non-routine problem solving:** A skilled problem-solver uses expert thinking to examine a broad span of information, recognize patterns, and narrow the information to reach a diagnosis of the problem. Moving beyond diagnosis to a solution requires knowledge of how the information is linked conceptually and involves metacognition—the ability to reflect on whether a problem-solving strategy is working and to switch to another strategy if the current strategy isn't working (Levy and Murnane, 2004). It includes creativity to generate new and innovative solutions, integrating seemingly unrelated information; and entertaining possibilities others may miss (Houston, 2007).

4. **Self-management/Self-development:** Self-management skills include the ability to work remotely, in virtual teams; to work autonomously; and to be self motivating and self monitoring. One aspect of self-management is the willingness and ability to acquire new information and skills related to work (Houston, 2007).

5. **Systems Thinking:** The ability to understand how an entire system works, how an action, change, or malfunction in one part of the system affects the rest of the system; adopting a "big picture" perspective on work (Houston, 2007). It includes judgment and decision-making;

systems analysis; and systems evaluation as well as abstract reasoning about how the different elements of a work process interact (Peterson, 1999).

- National Research Council Workshop on 21st Century Skills

Finally, a number of engineering education programs have already been introduced in schools (NAE, 2009). Although these programs are not based on national standards, they provide a critical entry point into the school system. Thus, there are many opportunities for engineering education, and the first step in realizing them is clarifying the purposes and developing the standards.

Barriers to the Development of Standards

There are few barriers to the development of standards for K–12 engineering education. With a sufficient budget, time, and expertise, the task of developing standards is clearly doable. There are, however, substantial barriers to realizing those standards in national and state education policies, school programs, and classroom practices. The education system into which the standards will be incorporated has very strong antibodies, to use a biological metaphor, that would be activated in the form of federal laws (e.g., No Child Left Behind), state standards and assessments, teachers' conceptual understanding and personal beliefs, instructional strategies, budget priorities, parental concerns, college and university teacher preparation programs, teacher unions, and the list goes on.

The power and position of science and mathematics in STEM education and the tendency to say STEM when one really means science or mathematics is a significant barrier. S, T, E, and M are separate but not equal. The inequality becomes clear, for example, when one considers that science, technology, and mathematics have national standards and that by 2012 all three will have national assessments. The National Assessment Governing Board (NAGB) approved a special national assessment of technological literacy for 2012, and work on the assessment framework is being coordinated by WestEd. Science and mathematics also figure prominently in international assessments, such as Trends in International Mathematics and Science Study (TIMSS) and Program for International Student Assessment (PISA).

A constellation of obstacles appears when one considers the educational infrastructure. For instance, state standards and assessments currently include only mathematics and science, which dominate the views of policy makers, school administrators, and classroom teachers. The financial situation for most states and school districts simply will not support the major changes in curriculum, instruction, and assessment that will be necessary for new national standards for engineering education.

Another potential problem is that national standards for the E in STEM could create another "silo." Because national standards for science, technology, and mathematics already exist and dominate the educational system, engineering education standards developed with little or no recognition of other STEM disciplines could be a disservice to STEM education, especially when one considers engineering's natural connections to science, technology, and mathematics.

Finally, engineering education has little leadership or political power to take advantage of critical leverage points in national, state, and local educational systems, such as international assessments, national assessments, state teacher certification requirements and teacher education programs, state standards and assessments, and programs for the professional development of current classroom teachers.

Final Reflections

Despite the significant barriers just described, the likelihood is high that the National Academies or some other agency or organization will develop content standards for K–12 engineering education. This likelihood is supported by a recent report, *Engineering in K–12 Education: Understanding the Status and Improving the Prospects* (NAE, 2009). The following suggestions may help inform the initial work.

First, should the standards be for K–12 engineering or for STEM literacy? This seems a critical initial decision. After review and consideration, I come down in favor of STEM literacy. This would avoid the "silo" problem, include engineering knowledge and design, place engineering in a leadership position, and provide a potential entry point into K–12 education. It would also promote an integrated approach to STEM programs (Van Scotter et al., 2000).

Second, the development of engineering education standards should be completed by a group that includes advisors, an oversight board, expert developers, engineers, educators, and classroom teachers. The goal is to develop standards with a "neutral" perspective that is not grounded in extant curricula, assessments, or projects.

Third, either specific engineering education standards or standards for STEM literacy will require content that represents the most important knowledge and skills for the subject(s).

Fourth, currently the question of what students should know and be able to do is a guide to decisions about content standards. We must understand the balance between learning outcomes for knowledge and learning outcomes for abilities.

Fifth, regardless of the path chosen, the content standards should address relationships among core academic disciplines—English, mathematics, science, and social studies.

Sixth, we must make the case that content standards for engineering are "world class" and suggest a positive contribution to international competitiveness.

Seventh, we must develop post-standard strategies to ensure that the standards have a positive and effective influence (NRC, 2002).

In conclusion, in this era of standards-based reform with the focus on STEM education, engineering has been ignored. Although there are significant opportunities to change the situation, this will require overcoming barriers, especially to the implementation of new standards. Developing them may be easy, but overcoming the implementation barriers will be difficult. Assuming an "if you build them, they will come" posture would be a fatal mistake. But we must seize the opportunity for the benefit of the nation, the education system, and especially the students in our schools.

References

American Association for the Advancement of Science (AAAS). 1989. Science for All Americans: A Project 2061 Report on Literacy Goals in Science, Mathematics, and Technology. Washington, DC: AAAS.

AAAS. 1993. Benchmarks for Scientific Literacy. New York: Oxford University Press.

Bybee, R., and Ferrini-Mundy, J. 1997. Guest Editorial. School Science and Mathematics 97(6): 281–282.

Collins, A. 1995. National science education standards in the United States: A process and a product. Studies in Science Education 26: 7-37.

DeBoer, G. 1991. A History of Ideas in Science Education. New York: Teachers College Press.

DeBoer, G. 2006. History of the Science Standards Movement in the United States. Pp. 7-49 in The Impact of State and National Standards on K–12 Science Teaching, edited by D. Sunal and E. Wright. New York: Information Age Publishing.

Engineering Concepts Curriculum Project. 1971. *The Man-Made World*. New York: McGraw-Hill Book Company.

Hiebert, J. 1999. Relationships between research and the NCTM standards. Journal for Research in Mathematics Education, 30(1): 3-19.

Holdren, J. 2009. Science in the White House. Science 324, 1 May, 2009.

Houston, J. 2007. Future skill demands, from a corporate consultant perspective. Presentation at the National Academies Workshop on Research Evidence Related to Future Skill Demands. Available online at *http://www7.nationalacademies.org/cfe/Future_Skill_ Demands_Presentations.html*. (September 13, 2010)

Hurd, P. 1999. Standards are fine, but they are not a reinvention. Education Week, November 24: 31.

International Technology Education Association (ITEA). 2000. Standards for technological literacy. Reston, Va: ITEA.

Levy, F., and R.J. Murnane. 2004. The New Division of Labor: How Computers Are Creating the Next Job Market. Princeton, NJ: Princeton University Press.

National Academy of Engineering. 2009. Engineering in K–12 Education: Understanding the Status and Improving the prospects. Edited by L. Katehi, G. Pearson, and M. Feder. Washington, DC: National Academies Press.

National Assessment Governing Board. 2008. Science Framework for the 2009 National Assessment of Educational Progress. Washington, D.C.: U.S. Department of Education.

National Commission on Excellence in Education. 1983. A Nation at Risk. Washington, D.C.: U.S. Government Printing Office.

National Council of Teachers of Mathematics (NCTM). 1989. Curriculum and Evaluation Standards for School Mathematics. Reston, Va: NCTM.

NCTM. 2000. Principles and Standards for School Mathematics. Reston, Va: NCTM.

National Research Council (NRC). 1996. National Science Education Standards. Washington, D.C.: National Academies Press.

NRC. 2002. Investigating the Influence of Standards. Washington, D.C.: National Academies Press.

Sanders, M. 2009. STEM, STEM education, STEM mania. The Technology Teacher 68 (4): 20-26. Reston, Va.: International Technology Education Association.

Sizer, T. 1964. Secondary Schools at the Turn of the Century. New Haven, Conn.: Yale University Press.

Van Scotter, P., Bybee, R., and Dougherty, M. 2000. Fundamentals of integrated science: what teachers should consider when planning an integrated science curriculum. The Science Teacher 67(6): 25–28.

**Formulating the Conceptual Base for Secondary Level Engineering Education:
A Review and Synthesis**
Rodney L. Custer, Jenny L. Daugherty, Joseph P. Meyer

Introduction

In recent years, there has been a growing interest in science, technology, engineering, and mathematics (STEM) education across the K-16 spectrum. While much of this interest has concentrated on science and mathematics, technology and engineering are emerging as authentic educational problem-solving contexts, as well as disciplines in their own right at the K–12 level. Over the past 20 years, the technology education field has concentrated on defining and implementing content standards, the *Standards for Technological Literacy* (ITEA, 2000) (the Standards), with mixed results. On a national scale, the field continues to evolve from its historical industrial arts base toward more contemporary approaches to curriculum and pedagogy. In spite of the publication of the Standards, which were designed to define the content base for technology education, practice continues to be driven by projects and activities with little focus on specific student learning outcomes. In addition, over the past decade, interest has shifted toward an alignment with engineering.

Corresponding with this shift in emphasis, the engineering profession has shown increasing interest in K–12 education. This interest can be largely attributed to a concern among engineering educators that too few students, including women and minorities, are being attracted to and prepared for post-secondary engineering education. More positively, there is a growing awareness that a well crafted engineering presence in the K–12 curriculum provides a rich contextual base for teaching and learning mathematics and science concepts. A variety of engineering-oriented programs have been developed, particularly at the secondary level, ranging from programs designed to promote general engineering/technological literacy (designed for all students) to programs designed to prepare students for post-secondary engineering education.

The National Center for Engineering and Technology Education (NCETE) has undertaken a larger scale initiative focused on pre-college engineering. NCETE was funded in 2004 through the National Science Foundation (NSF) Centers for Learning and Teaching Program. Over the past five years, a consortium of nine universities, through NCETE, has engaged in a variety of activities, including teacher professional development, the preparation of a cohort of doctoral students, and research. In the past year, NCETE's activities have focused more directly on research.

One key problem that has emerged from NCETE's work is the lack of a well defined, well articulated body of content for K–12 engineering education. This void poses serious problems for curriculum and professional development, as well as for research. Specifically, high quality curricular materials must be based on a well defined set of concepts and content. In the absence of this content base, materials tend to feature engaging activities that do not necessarily focus on conceptual learning or have the rigor necessary for accountability. The same problem occurs with professional development and pre-service teacher education. High quality teacher preparation and development must be congruent with a well defined base of content and concepts.

The absence of a clear understanding of the conceptual and content base appropriate for K–12 engineering education makes the development of meaningful learning, teaching, and assessment exceptionally problematic. The present study is designed to address this void.

Fortunately, interest in K–12 engineering over the past decade has yielded a variety of activities, projects, and products that can inform the process. Among these are various science, technology, engineering, and mathematics (STEM) standards, engineering-oriented curricula, studies by the National Academy of Engineering, and research on engineering learning outcomes appropriate for K–12 students. Given these activities and the need for a well defined concept base as a foundation for curriculum, professional development, and research, it is time we had a study to coalesce and refine the conceptual base for engineering education at the K–12 level.

Purpose of Study

The purpose of the present study was to identify and refine a conceptual foundation for secondary school engineering education. The study attempts to address the following research questions:

1. What engineering concepts are present in literature related to the nature and philosophy of engineering?
2. What engineering concepts are embedded in secondary level science, technology, engineering, and mathematics standards?
3. What engineering concepts are embedded in secondary level engineering-oriented curricula?
4. What engineering concepts have been identified in the research literature?
5. What engineering concepts are considered to be core concepts for secondary level education by practicing engineers and engineering educators?

Key input for the study comes from a review and synthesis of extant educational materials focused primarily on standards, curricular materials, and research. In addition to these materials, literature from the history and philosophy of engineering was reviewed and included in the analysis. A series of focus group sessions was held with selected engineering educators and practicing engineers to identify and classify their recommendations for concepts appropriate to secondary level engineering education. As a final phase of the process, a reaction and validation panel will meet in late July 2009.

Literature Review/Theoretical Foundations

Numerous reasons have been cited for including engineering in K–12 education. Erekson and Custer (2008) summarized three of them: engineering would help to (a) facilitate technological literacy, (b) provide a learning context for math and science, and (c) enhance an engineering pathway. These three principles have spurred the growth of engineering education at the K–12 level. For example, a 2007 NSF review of engineering education identified numerous K–12 engineering programs including: (a) projects at Worcester Polytechnic Institute and the University of Colorado at Boulder; (b) curricular programs, such as *The Infinity Project* and *Project Lead the Way*; (c) business-oriented programs, such as the Ford Partnership for Advanced Students; and (d) competitions, such as the For Inspiration and Recognition of Science and Technology's Robotics Competition. Based on that review of K–12 programs, the authors of the report concluded that there are "many faces of engineering K–12 curriculum" (Aung et al., 2007, p. 27).

To help educators looking for ways to integrate engineering into secondary level education, we must first define K–12 engineering content. Many involved in technology education have argued for the engineering design process as the avenue for integration (Lewis, 2005; Wicklein, 2006). Thus, the discussion about integrating engineering design into technology education has largely centered on process or "problem solving and the application of scientific understanding to a given task" (Hill and Anning, 2001, p. 118). Many instructors have taught engineering design problem solving by implementing a prescriptive, step-by-step approach, typically through a design process model. However, the prescriptive approach to teaching design has been increasingly criticized because it contradicts both expert and novice designers' approaches to the problem solving and design process (Lewis et al., 1998; Mawson, 2003; Welch, 1999; Williams, 2000).

Based on the evidence of the importance of conceptual knowledge in expert design cognition, the lack of a defined content base and the focus on procedural knowledge raises concerns. This same argument has been thoroughly discussed in mathematics, where a focus on process does not always lead to conceptual learning (Eisenhart et al., 1993; Rittle-Johnson and Alibali, 1999; Rittle-Johnson et al., 2001). For example, Antony (1996) argued that teachers "may be lulled into a false sense of security by providing students with numerous investigations, open-ended problem-solving experiences, and hands-on activities with the expectations that students are successfully constructing knowledge from these experiences" (p. 351). The crucial importance of conceptual learning calls into question educational programs that try "to focus on procedural knowledge such as problem solving or design, while assuming that the domain and context within which this takes place are either irrelevant or at best secondary" (McCormick, 1997, p. 149).

In addition, the effectiveness of teacher professional development has been shown to depend on a defined content base. As Guskey (2003) stated, enabling "teachers to understand more deeply the content they teach and the ways students learn that content appears to be a vital dimension of effective professional development" (p. 749). Desimone et al. (2002) agreed, arguing that high quality professional development must include "a focus on content and how students learn content, in-depth" (p. 82). Similarly, Supovitz and Turner (2000) outlined components of high quality science education professional development and concluded that focusing on subject-matter knowledge and deepening teachers' content skills were critical. Specific to engineering professional development, one key finding of Daugherty's (2008) study on secondary level, engineering-focused professional development was that the content dimension was either ill-defined or largely missing. The primary focus was on the process dimensions of engineering rather than on engineering content or concepts.

Content and Conceptual Learning
Learning can be defined as the social construction of knowledge. Individuals construct schemata, or knowledge structures, through experience and instruction. Schemata impact the learning of new concepts or theories, as well as "give experts in a domain the ability to solve problems quickly" (McCormick, 1997, p. 148). Concepts form the basis of conceptual knowledge, which is "formed in memory by the integrated storage of meaningful dimensions selected from known examples and the connecting of this entity in a given domain of information" (Tennyson and Cocchiarella, 1986, p. 41). Unlike declarative knowledge, conceptual knowledge requires an understanding of the operational structure of something and how it relates to associated concepts. A concept can be defined as "an abstract label that encompasses an array of diverse instances deemed to be related" (Sigel, 1983, p. 242). Similarly,

Erickson (2002) described a concept as an organizing idea that is timeless, universal, abstract and broad, represented by one or two words, and examples of which share common attributes. Conceptual knowledge can be "thought of as a connected web of knowledge, a network in which the linking relationships are as prominent as the discrete pieces of information" (Hiebert and Lefevre, 1986, p. 3-4).

Erickson (2002) argued that attempting to "teach in the 21st century without a conceptual schema for knowledge is like trying to build a house without a blueprint" (p. 7). Bransford and Donavon (2005) concurred, arguing that the clarity of the core concepts of the discipline "is required if students are to grasp what the discipline—history, math, or science—is about" (p. 576). Teaching for conceptual understanding requires that the core concepts that organize the knowledge of experts also organize instruction. Donavon and Bransford (2005) concluded that this approach to teaching has two parts: "(1) factual knowledge (e.g., about characteristics of different species) must be placed in a conceptual framework (about adaptation) to be well understood; and (2) concepts are given meaning by multiple representations that are rich in factual detail" (p. 6). Thus concepts do not stand alone but "take on meaning in the knowledge-rich contexts in which they are applied" (p. 6).

According to Bransford et al. (2000), in order to "develop competence in an area of inquiry, students must: (a) have a deep foundation of factual knowledge, (b) understand facts and ideas in the context of a conceptual framework, and (c) organize knowledge in ways that facilitate retrieval and application" (p. 16). They added that this "will require both a deepening of the information base and the development of a conceptual framework for that subject matter" (p. 17). In addition, conceptual frameworks allow for greater learning transfer because they give students opportunities to apply what they have learned to new situations and to learn related information more quickly. Tennyson and Cocchiarella (1986) outlined an instructional design approach to conceptual teaching. They characterized the process of teaching concepts as threefold: (a) establishing a connection between the to-be-learned concept and specific necessary knowledge; (b) improving the formation of the conceptual knowledge by elaborating further the schematic structure of relational concepts; and (c) improving development of procedural knowledge skills. This approach to instruction means there is "a need to establish criteria for delineating the content boundaries of a concept" (Sigel, 1983, p. 243).

McCormick (1997) argued that when "concepts are introduced in school, they are not transmitted to students, but students will attempt to fit them to the models or concepts they currently have" (p. 148). This constructivist view of conceptual learning challenges teachers introducing technological activities to identify the possible knowledge requirements of technology tasks, ascertain students' relevant prior knowledge, and provide adequate support for conceptual development. Activities such as design, modeling, problem solving, system approaches, project planning, quality assurance, and optimization "are all candidates for technological procedural knowledge, and can be found across many technologies whatever their specific context" (McCormick, 1997, p. 144). However, the specific context is important in the development of technological knowledge because it requires specific domain knowledge. For example, problem-solving skills are "dependent upon considerable domain knowledge" (McCormick, 1997, p. 146), not simply procedural knowledge. In addition, "it is the possession of conceptual knowledge that makes possible the effective use of the procedural knowledge of problem solving" (McCormick, 1997, p. 149).

The understanding of process or procedural knowledge is related to technological knowledge. Costa and Liebmann (1997) argued that content should be seen in terms of how it enhances the development of processes. Process requires the learning of content; each "piece of subject matter is a way of knowing, a way of representing, or a way of solving problems" (Costa and Liebemann, 1997, p. 14). Processes may be thought of on three levels: (a) skills, (b) operations, and (c) dispositions. Skills are discrete and include mental functions, such as comparing and classifying. Operations, which are larger strategies employed over time, require clusters of skills. Dispositions are habits of mind, inclinations, and proclivities. Although procedural knowledge is crucial to learning, it cannot be taught in isolation from conceptual knowledge.

Method

The present qualitative study was conducted by a team of three researchers with diverse experiences in secondary school engineering education. When conducting qualitative research, it is important to specify and reference researchers' backgrounds and qualifications, because backgrounds and experiences provide "lenses" through which the outcomes are generated and reflected upon (Malterud, 2001). Dr. Rodney L. Custer has been extensively involved in standards, curriculum, and professional development. His formal academic work includes an industrial engineering cognate in the Ph.D. program and degrees in education, psychology, and theology. He has served on several National Academy of Engineering studies focused on technological literacy and was a program officer at NSF. Dr. Jenny L. Daugherty has been a curriculum specialist on an engineering-oriented secondary level curriculum project, has conducted several national teacher engineering-oriented workshops, and has been involved in numerous funded projects focused on K–12 STEM education. Along with a firm grasp of the issues involved in secondary level engineering education, she also has a broad liberal-arts perspective based on her B.A. in history and sociology and M.A. in history. Joe Meyer worked as a civil engineer before pursuing a master's degree in science education and teaching secondary math and science. Thus he is familiar with the technical and professional aspects of engineering as well as the institutional, social, and curricular challenges of teaching secondary level math and science students.

The primary data were collected for this study in the following ways: (a) a review of extant documents; and (b) focus groups. The review of extant documents evolved from initial data collection as the researchers prepared for the first focus group. To provide a framework for the focus groups, they conducted a thorough review of the literature on the philosophical underpinnings of engineering and technology. Ultimately, four sets of documents were reviewed: (a) literature on engineering and technology philosophy; (b) curricular materials focused on secondary level engineering; (c) curricular standards documents developed for STEM disciplines and relevant National Academy of Engineering reports; and (d) Delphi research studies relevant to K–12 engineering.

Review of Extant Documents

The goal of the document review was to systematically identify and review key documents on core engineering concepts. The selection of documents for analysis varied. The philosophical literature was selected by a researcher whose doctoral dissertation included a thorough treatment of the philosophy of engineering and technology. Curricular materials were drawn from those identified as appropriate for secondary level engineering education by Dr. Ken Welty, University of Wisconsin, Stout, who conducted a curriculum analysis that was included in a recent report on K–12 engineering education (NAE and NRC, 2009). Only modules and units directly related to engineering were reviewed. The standards documents included in the review were developed by the professional organizations representing the STEM disciplines. The Delphi research studies were identified through searches of electronic databases and were selected based on their research orientation and relevance to secondary level engineering education.

The review of engineering and technology philosophy included: *Engineering Philosophy* (Bucciarelli, 2003); *Thinking Through Technology: The Path Between Engineering and Philosophy* (Mitcham, 1999); *The Introspective Engineer* (Florman, 1996); *Engineering as Productive Activity* (Mitcham, 1991); *The Social Captivity of Engineering* (Goldman, 1991); *The Eco-philosophy Approach to Technological Research* (Skolimowski, 1991); *Deficiencies in Engineering Education* (Ropohl, 1991); *What Engineers Know and How They Know It* (Vincenti, 1990); *Ethics Engineering* (Martin and Schinzinger, 1996); *Discussion of the Method: Conducting the Engineer's Approach to Problem Solving* (Koen, 2003); *Autonomous Technology* (Winner, 1977); and *Technology as Knowledge* (Layton, 1974).

The curricula included for analysis were: *A World in Motion* (SAE International); *Design and Discovery* (Intel Corporation); *Materials World*; *Engineering by Design*; *Engineering the Future*; *Exploring Design and Engineering*; *Ford Partnership for Advanced Students*; *INSPIRES*; *Project Lead the Way*; and *The Infinity Project*. The curriculum standards reviewed for this study included: *Benchmarks for Science Literacy* (AAAS, 1993/2009), *Criteria for Accrediting Engineering Programs* (ABET, 2000), *National Science Education Standards*, (NRC, 1996), *Principles and Standards for School Mathematics* (NCTM, 2000), *Standards for Technological Literacy* (ITEA, 2000). In addition, the 2005 National Academy of Engineering study, *The Engineer of 2020*, was also reviewed. The five Delphi research studies reviewed were: (a) Childress and Rhodes (2008); (b) Harris and Rogers (2008); (c) Childress and Sanders (2007); (d) Smith (2006); and (e) Dearing and Daugherty (2004).

The researchers developed a standard process for reviewing each set of documents, which was reviewed by two of the three researchers. The reviewers identified "engineering themes" in the narrative, that is, elements in the narrative that were described as important to engineering and applicable across various engineering disciplines. At this stage in the process, the decision was made to be inclusive and identify themes that would later be analyzed and refined through a systematic, analytic procedure by the research team. Each reviewer recorded the theme, supporting narrative, and page number in a table. After the independent reviews were completed, the results were compared and differences were reconciled.

From the preliminary list of engineering themes, all three researchers independently rated what they considered to be core engineering concepts. To the extent possible, the reviewers selected concepts distinct from the more "process-oriented skills" and "social/interpersonal disposition" aspects of engineering. The three lists were then compared for continuity and subjected to criteria to meet the following established definitions of "engineering," "core," and "concepts":

- Engineering: defined by the Accreditation Board for Engineering and Technology (ABET) as the knowledge of the mathematical and natural sciences, gained by study, experience, and practice, is applied with judgment to develop ways to use, economically, the materials and forces for the benefit of mankind (Gomez et al., 2006). The research team focused specifically on the study, expertise, and practice specific to engineering education and experience.

- Concepts: abstract labels; organizing ideas; typically represented with one or two words; take on meaning in the knowledge-rich contexts in which they are applied (Erickson, 2002; Hiebert and Lefevre, 1986; Sigel, 1983; Tennyson and Cocchiarella, 1986). The research team concentrated on the robustness and complexity of ideas, where the ideas could be "unpacked," and where they extended well beyond procedural matters.
- Core: The center of an object; a small group of indispensable things; and the most essential or most vital part of some idea or experience (Wordnet, 2009).

Focus Groups

In addition to the review of documents, the researchers conducted three focus group sessions with engineering educators and practicing engineers. The purpose of these sessions, which was closely aligned with the document-based review, was to capture participants' thinking about engineering concepts distinct from the process and interpersonal aspects of engineering. Several factors contributed to the importance of the focus groups. First, very few, if any, of the documents reviewed were specifically designed to identify engineering concepts. As a result, the synthesis involved "teasing" concepts from materials developed for other purposes. Second, the focus groups gave the researchers a chance to probe the thinking of individuals with demonstrated ability to think broadly and conceptually about engineering practice and engineering education. In contrast to the more indirect approach in the document review, the focus groups provided a structured, direct approach to identifying concepts.

The focus groups consisted of engineering education faculty and practicing engineers from selected departments of engineering and local engineering firms. A point person at each university familiar with the issues involved in secondary level engineering education identified individuals to participate in the focus groups based on guidance from the research team. The goal was to identify individuals with a recognized interest and expertise in broad, conceptual aspects of engineering as well as an interest in secondary level education. The faculty selected to participate in the focus groups taught entry level, orientation-type engineering courses, which were designed to be general and did not focus on content specific to any one engineering discipline. Practicing engineers were selected based on their ability to think broadly about engineering education. One focus group session was held at Colorado State University, and two were held at Virginia Tech University.

The focus group sessions were held concurrent with the analysis of the philosophical documents. To facilitate the discussions, the researchers used an affinity group process technique, which consists of three steps. First, participants were provided with an orientation to characterize engineering concepts and explain how they differ from process and interpersonal skills. Each individual was then given five minutes to identify and write concepts onto sticky notes (one concept per sticky). The notes were then placed on a large wall for display and review, and the group was led through a process of clustering concepts into categories, which was followed by naming each category by group consensus. As a group, the participants then eliminated redundancies by placing duplicates on top of each other to retain frequencies. Second, the group classified concepts into three columns: (a) core concepts of engineering; (b) concepts on the fringe of engineering; and (c) concepts in an intermediate category. And third, when this classification was complete, the groups identified each concept as: (a) doing; or (b) knowing.

Remaining Activities

The culminating activity of the study will consist of a validation/reaction process conducted by a focus group in late July 2009. The purposes of this phase of the study will be to (a) provide a context for the findings of the review and focus groups and (b) refine and structure the list of concepts generated through the review and synthesis activities by the focus groups (i.e., key stakeholders in secondary level engineering education). Participants will be selected based on their recognized ability to think conceptually, their knowledge of secondary level education, and their understanding of the engineering profession. A goal of this purposeful selection of participants will be to ensure that both STEM education and industry are represented.

The focus group will be engage in a two-part process designed to compare and contrast the outcomes of the review and synthesis with the group's own expertise and thinking. In the first part, participants will be led through the same concept-identification process used for the earlier focus groups. In addition to generating concepts and framing the goals of the investigation, this first activity will help familiarize participants with the process used for previous groups. The second activity will lead participants through a series of discussions designed to analyze the group output in light of the synthesized findings from the study to date.

Findings

The researchers' findings comprised a synthesis of five major analyses including: (a) key history and philosophy of engineering and technology documents; (b) focus groups, (c) curriculum materials; (d) standards documents; and (e) Delphi studies on identifying engineering and technological outcomes. The five analyses yielded an extensive list of more than 100 themes the research team considered pertinent to engineering. Each member of the team independently applied the three criteria central to the analysis to each theme (i.e., core, engineering, and concepts) to all of five sets of materials. Then the team met and engaged in extensive discussions to compare ratings and arrive at a consensus on the items that met all three criteria. This process generated a list of core engineering concepts for each set of materials. After consensus was achieved, a composite list of concepts for all five sets of materials was compiled. Figure 1 shows the 14 concepts generated through this process and provides brief descriptions and an indication which of the five input sources applies. It should be noted that the descriptions are directly based on terminology used in documents throughout the analysis.

Concept	Description	Curriculum	Philosophy	Standards	Focus Groups	Delphi Studies
design	iterative, technological, analysis based, experimental, ergonomic, universal	•	•	•	•	•
modeling	mathematical, computer-based, sketching, technical drawing, physical	•	•	•	•	•
constraints	criteria, specifications, limitations, requirements	•	•	•	•	•
innovation	creativity, improvement, refinement, invention	•	•	•	•	•
systems	input/output, process, feedback, component design and interaction, subsystems	•	•	•	•	•
optimization	improvement, refinement, balancing, decision heuristics	•	•	•	•	•
experimentation	testing, test development, trial and error	•	•	•	•	•
prototyping	physical and process modeling and evaluation, preliminary	•	•	•	•	•
trade-offs	conflicting constraints, negotiation, competing requirements or criteria	•	•	•	•	•
analysis	risk, cost/benefit, life-cycle, failure, mathematical, decision, functional, economic	•	•	•	•	•
problem solving	description of need, solution generation, troubleshooting, invention, design	•	•	•	•	•
functionality	key engineering goal, usefulness, practicality	•	•		•	•
visualization	imagery, spatial and abstract representation, sketching	•	•	•		•
efficiency	key engineering goal, guiding principle	•	•	•		

Figure 1 Composite List of Core Engineering Concepts

It is important to note that, although the researchers' goal was to identify core engineering concepts appropriate to secondary level engineering education, the team was also interested in larger issues and implications associated with the process. This type of reflective discussion is consistent with how themes, issues, and outcomes emerge from qualitative research and data analysis. To capture these ideas, the team maintained reflective notes throughout the review and synthesis process. These notes have been compiled and will be presented as part of the conclusions and implications section of this manuscript.

As Figure1 shows, there was remarkable conceptual consistency among the five major inputs. Eleven of the 14 concepts were represented in all five inputs, and two concepts were represented in four of the five. It is also clear that there is considerable conceptual overlap and interaction among the concepts. For example, many, if not most, represent elements or aspects of the engineering design process. This conceptual overlap makes sense given the interconnected nature of engineering design.

It should also be noted that the list in Figure 1 is a distillation of a longer list of more than 100 themes, a substantial number of which were judged to meet the "core" and "engineering" criteria, but not the "conceptual" criterion. Although these themes are important to engineering, the goal of this study was to identify ideas judged to be the most conceptually robust.

Discussion and Implications

The review and synthesis process used for this study generated a list of core engineering concepts appropriate for the curricular and professional development needs of secondary level engineering educators. On a larger scale, the outcomes of the study include much more than a definitive list of core engineering concepts. The difficult questions raised throughout the process about the nature of engineering epistemology, the purpose of engineering education on the secondary level, and the applicability of concepts throughout the K-16 spectrum are equally important. These issues are discussed in this section.

One important issue raised throughout the analysis had to do with the purpose of teaching engineering at the secondary level. At one extreme, secondary-level engineering can be considered pre-college education for students preparing for engineering courses on the college level. At the other extreme, secondary-level engineering education that provides general knowledge about engineering and how things are designed is appropriate, and even necessary, to preparing all students to live in a technologically rich culture. The issues raised in this study are whether the same concepts considered appropriate/important to engineering are also appropriate for both pre-engineering and general literacy. A related issue is whether the engineering concepts appropriate for secondary level education are applicable throughout the K–12 spectrum.

At a number of points in the analysis, it was apparent that engineering design is a central and dominant conceptual theme. In some of the documents, particularly the curricular materials, the focus was clearly on engineering design. The steps in the engineering design process (e.g., problem formulation, brainstorming, prototyping) were considered the framework for teaching engineering. In other documents and in the focus groups, the discussion dealt with other aspects of engineering (e.g., functionality, efficiency, systems, and optimization). Although these aspects can also be considered to be subsumed by engineering design, they were presented as more robust concepts independent of the steps in the engineering design process. Thus, design can be considered the primary engineering concept or even a threshold concept (Meyer and Land, 2006). A threshold concept differs from a core concept in that it is "akin to a portal, opening up a new and previously inaccessible way of thinking about something" (p. 3). Engineering design could provide the "portal" for all other engineering concepts and themes appropriate for K–12 students.

Throughout the analysis, the research team struggled with defining an engineering epistemology and conceptual base that is appropriate only to engineering. The researchers struggled to identify concepts and knowledge that related strictly and distinctly to engineering. The team concluded that doing so was problematic for two primary reasons. First, the engineering field includes a spectrum of disciplines, each of which tends to draw on knowledge specific to that discipline. For example, the knowledge base for nuclear engineering is distinct from the knowledge base for civil engineering; each discipline has a pool of knowledge necessary to conduct activities and analyses specific to that field. The question was whether engineering disciplines have a common conceptual core that can be generalized across disciplines. The second problem with conceptualizing an engineering epistemology is that much of engineering is grounded in and interwoven with knowledge from other academic disciplines, particularly science and mathematics. The same problem arises with respect to technology, namely, that technological knowledge is essentially derived from the application of knowledge from other disciplines.

The issue of engineering knowledge extends beyond epistemology to "engineering practice" and "engineering dispositions." This became clear in the focus group discussions where attempts were made to draw distinctions between concepts that engineers primarily know and those they primarily do. Given the applied, socially grounded, contextual nature of engineering practice, these are interesting distinctions. As Childress and Sanders (2007) pointed out, the *ABET Criteria 2000* emphasize teaching dispositions, such as communication and lifelong learning, instead of specific engineering concepts. A directly related issue is that social science issues continually emerged during the analysis of engineering-related documents. Primary among these were the social context for engineering, ethics, and interpersonal skills. Although these did not meet the criteria for core engineering concepts established for this study, engineering activity is clearly grounded in a larger system that reflects values, needs, and impacts on societies and cultures. Engineering and technology are inherently social constructs (Bijker et al., 1989), and contextual issues must be taken into consideration for core engineering concepts to be formulated and understood in a meaningful way.

Two additional conceptual distinctions emerged in the analysis. These have to do with the nature of problem solving and experimentation. First, problem solving emerged as a substantial theme in all five data sets. This makes sense given the fundamental nature of engineering design. Activities ranging from the clarification of design parameters relative to (often competing) design constraints to problems associated with translating engineering theory into practical outcomes all involve solving problems. Thus, on the level of practical implementation, a compelling case can be made for including problem solving as a fundamental engineering concept. On the conceptual level, however, several other issues emerged. First, when problem solving is viewed generically, it extends far beyond engineering and technological activities. For example, in the social sciences, problem solving applies to everything from international relations to community relations to personal mental health issues (Custer, 1995). In fact, problem solving has been classified in three major categories based on Newell and Simon's (1972) notion of problem space. The three problem spaces, defined in terms of activity goals, include personal/social, scientific, and technological. Another issue pertinent to engineering is whether problem solving represents an overarching concept that subsumes design, invention, and troubleshooting (Custer, 1995).

Experimentation, like problem solving, emerged as a strong theme throughout the analysis. Two issues were raised in discussions about including it as a core engineering concept. First, the term "experimentation" is closely identified with science and the scientific method. In a scientific context, experimentation connotes a specific methodology for establishing and testing hypotheses with the goal of developing a theory. In an engineering context, experimentation has more to do generally with incremental trial and error in making a design work (e.g., extending human capabilities and meeting needs and wants). Thus, the argument can be made that the term experimentation is more appropriately associated with science than with engineering. A related issue is the extent to which engineering is considered as science and, as a consequence, whether experimentation represents a formal analysis of applications of engineering theory.

Concluding Comments

The purpose of the study described in this paper was to identify a conceptual foundation for secondary level engineering education. It should be apparent that this was a daunting task that raised a number of associated conceptual and practical issues that have implications for the serious consideration of engineering as an integral part of the K–12 curriculum. These issues could significantly impact educational policy at the pre-college level where the case remains to be made for including engineering content, as well as at the post-secondary level where there are increasing calls for reform in engineering education. Areas that warrant further investigation include the possible need for K–12 engineering standards, curricula, and teacher pre-service and professional development. The central premise of this study is that these issues should be addressed after the conceptual foundations have been carefully and thoughtfully developed.

References

Accreditation Board for Engineering and Technology, Inc. (ABET). (2000). *Criteria for accrediting engineering programs, http://www.abet.org/.*

American Association for the Advancement of Science (AAAS). (1993/2009). *Benchmarks for science literacy.* Project 2061. New York: Oxford University Press.

Antony, G. (1996). Active learning in a constructivist framework. *Educational Studies in Mathematics, 31*(4), 349-369.

Aung, W., Kwasiborksi, V., & Soyster, A. L. (2007). A review of engineering education 1998-2007. Division of Engineering Education and Centers, Directorate for Engineering, National Science Foundation.

Bijker, W., Hughes, T. P., & Pinch, T. (1989). *The social construction of technological systems.* Boston, MA: MIT Press.

Bransford, J. D., Brown, A. L., & Cocking, R. R. (Eds.). (2000). *How people learn: Brain, mind, experience, and school.* Washington, DC: National Academy Press.

Bransford, J. D., & Donavon, M. S. (2005). Scientific inquiry and how people learn. In M. S. Donavon, & J. D. Bransford (Eds.). *How Students Learn: History, Mathematics, and Science in the Classroom* (pp. 397-419). Washington, DC: National Academies Press.

Bucciarelli, L. L. (2003). *Engineering philosophy.* Delft University Press: The Netherlands.

Childress, V., & Rhodes, C. (2008). Engineering student outcomes for grades 9-12. *The Technology Teacher, 5*(7), 5-12.

Childress, V., & Sanders, M. (2007). Core engineering concepts foundational for the study of technology in grades 6-12. In R. Custer (Ed.). *Professional development for engineering and technology: A national symposium,* February 2007. Retrieved September 03, 2008, http://www.conferences.ilstu.edu/NSA/homepage.html.

Costa, A. L., & Liebmann, R. M. (1997). Toward renaissance curriculum: An idea whose time has come. In A. L. Costa, & R. M. Liebmann. (Eds.). *Envisioning process as content: Toward a renaissance curriculum* (pp. 1 – 20). Thousand Oaks, CA: Corwin.

Custer, R. L. (1995). Examining the dimensions of technology. *International Journal of Technology and Design Education, 5*(5), 219-244.

Daugherty, J. L. (2008). *Engineering-oriented professional development for secondary level teachers: A multiple case study analysis.* Unpublished doctoral dissertation. University of Illinois, Urbana-Champaign.

Dearing, B. M., & Daugherty, M. K. (2004). Delivering engineering content in technology education. *The Technology Teacher, 64*(3), 8-11.

Desimone, L. M., Porter, A. C., Garet, M. S., Yoon, K. S., & Birman, B. F. (2002). Effects of professional development on teachers' instruction: Results from a three-year longitudinal study. *Educational Evaluation and Policy Analysis, 24*(2), 81-112.

Eisenhart, M., Borko, H., Underhill, R., Brown, C., Jones, D., & Agard, P. (1993). Conceptual knowledge falls through the cracks: Complexities of learning to teach mathematics for understanding. *Journal for Research in Mathematics Education, 24*(1), 8-40.

Erekson, T. L., & Custer, R. L. (2008). Conceptual foundations: Engineering and technology education. In R. L. Custer, & T. L. Erekson. *Engineering and technology education.* 57th Yearbook, Council on Technology Teacher Education (pp. 1-12). Woodland Hills, CA: Glencoe.

Erickson, H. L. (2002). *Concept-based curriculum and instruction: Teaching beyond the facts.* Thousand Oaks, CA: Corwin.

Florman, S. (1996). *The introspective engineer*. New York: St Martin's Press.

Goldman, S. L. (1991). The social captivity of engineering. In P. T. Durbin (Ed.), *Critical perspectives on non academic Science and Engineering*, Lehigh University Press, Bethlehem, PA.

Gomez, A. G., Oakes, W. C., & Leone, L. L. (2006). *Engineering your future: A project-based introduction to engineering*. 2nd ed. Wildwood, MO: Great Lakes Press.

Guskey, T. (2003). What makes professional development effective? *Phi Delta Kappan 84*, 748-750.

Harris, K. S., & Rogers, G. E. (2008). Secondary engineering competencies: A Delphi study of engineering faculty. *Journal of Industrial Teacher Education, 45*(1), 5-25.

Hiebert, J., & Lefevre, P. 1986. Conceptual and procedural knowledge in mathematics: An introductory analysis. In J. Hiebert (Ed.). *Conceptual and procedural knowledge: The case of mathematics* (pp. 1-27). Hillsdale, NJ: Lawrence Erlbaum.

Hill, A. M., & Anning, A. (2001). Primary teachers' and students' understanding of school situated design in Canada and England. *Research in Science Education, 31*(1), 117-135.

International Technology Education Association (ITEA). (2000). *Standards for technological literacy: Content for the study of technology*. Reston, VA

Koen, B. V. (2003). *Discussion of the Method: Conducting the Engineer's Approach to Problem Solving*. New York, NY: Oxford University Press.

Layton, E. T. (1974). Technology as knowledge. *Technology and Culture, 15*(1), 31-41.

Lewis, T. (2005). Coming to terms with engineering design as content. *Journal of Technology Education, 16*(2), 37-54.

Lewis, T., Petrina, S., & Hill, A. M. (1998). Problem posing: Adding a creative increment to technological problem solving. *Journal of Industrial Teacher Education, 36*(1), 5-35.

Malterud, K. (2001). Qualitative research: Standards, challenges, and guidelines. *The Lancet, 358*, 483-488.

Martin M.W. & Schinzinger R (1996), *Ethics in engineering*. 3rd ed. New York: McGraw-Hill.

Mawson, B. (2003). Beyond 'The Design Process': An Alternative pedagogy for technology education. *International Journal of Design Education, 13*(2), 117-128.

McCormick, R. (1997). Conceptual and procedural knowledge. *International Journal of Technology and Design Education, 7*, 141-159.

Meyer, J. H. F. & Land, R. (2006). Threshold concepts and troublesome knowledge: Linkages to ways of thinking and practising within the disciplines. In J. H. F. Meyer & R. Land, (Eds.). *Overcoming barriers to student understanding: Threshold concepts and troublesome knowledge* (pp. 3-18). London: Routledge Falmer.

Mitcham, C. (1991). Engineering as productive activity: Philosophical remarks. In P. T. Durbin (Ed.). *Critical perspectives on nonacademic science and engineering. Research in Technology Studies*, Vol. 4. London and Toronto: Associated University Press.

Mitcham, C. (1999), *Thinking through technology: The path between engineering and philosophy*. Chicago: University of Chicago Press.

National Academy of Engineering (NAE). (2005). *The engineer of 2020: Adapting engineering education to the new century*. Washington, DC: National Academy Press.

NAE and NRC (National Academy of Engineering and National Research Council). (2009) Engineering in K–12 Education: Understanding the Status and Improving the Prospects. Washington, D.C.: National Academies Press.

National Council Teachers of Mathematics (NCTM). (2000). *Principles and standards for school mathematics*. Reston, VA: NCTM.

National Research Council (NRC). (1996) *National science education standards*, Washington DC: National Academy Press.

Newell, A., & Simon, H. (1972). *Human problem solving*. Englewood Cliffs, NJ: Prentice-Hall.

Rittle-Johnson, B., & Alibali, M. W. (1999). Conceptual and procedural knowledge of mathematics: Does one lead to the other? *Journal of Educational Psychology, 91*(1), 175-189.

Rittle-Johnson, B., Siegler, R. S., & Alibali, M. W. (2001). Developing conceptual understanding and procedural skill in mathematics: An iterative process. *Journal of Educational Psychology, 93*(2), 346-362.

Ropohl, G. (1991). *Deficiencies in engineering education*. In P. T. Durbin (Ed.). *Critical Perspectives on Nonacademic Science and Engineering. Research in Technology Studies*, Vol. 4. London and Toronto: Associated University Press.

Sigel, I. E. (1983). Is the concept of the concept still elusive or what do we know about concept development? In E. K. Scholnick (Ed.). *New trends in conceptual representation: Challenges to Piaget's theory?* Hillsdale, NJ: Lawrence Erlbaum.

Skolimowski, H. (1991). The eco-philosophy approach to technological research. In P. T. Durbin (Ed.). *Critical Perspectives on Nonacademic Science and Engineering. Research in Technology Studies*, Vol. 4. London and Toronto: Associated University Press.

Smith, P. C. (2006). *Essential aspects and related academic concepts of an engineering design curriculum in secondary technology education.* Unpublished doctoral dissertation. University of Georgia, Urbana-Champaign.

Supovitz, J., & Turner, H. (2000). The effects of professional development on science teaching practices and classroom culture. *Journal of Research in Science Teaching, 37*(9), 963-980.

Tennyson, R. D., & Cocchiarella, M. J. (1986). An empirically based instructional design theory for teaching concepts. *Review of Educational Research, 56*(1), 40-71.

Vincenti, W. G. (1990). *What engineers know and how they know it: Analytical studies from aeronautical history*. Baltimore, MD: Johns Hopkins University Press.

Welch, M. (1999). Analyzing the tacit strategies of novice designers. *Research in Science & Technological Education, 17*(1), 19-34.

Wicklein, R. C. (2006). Five good reasons for engineering design as the focus for technology education. *The Technology Teacher, 65*(7), 25-29.

Williams, P. J. (2000). Design: The only methodology of technology?" *Journal of Technology Education, 11*(2), 48-60.

Winner, L. (1977). *Autonomous technology: Technics-out-of-control as a theme in political thought*. M.I.T. Press, Cambridge, MA.

Wordnet. Definitions of core on the web, Retrieved March 14, 2009, http://wordnet.princeton.edu/perl/webwn.

Report for NAE on Non-U.S. Standards for Pre-University Engineering Education

Marc J. de Vries
Delft University of Technology/Eindhoven University of Technology
The Netherlands

1. Background of the Report

As part of an ongoing project, the National Academies has studied pre-university engineering initiatives, with a focus on curriculum. Part of that project was a survey of non-U.S. initiatives. The emphasis in the report I wrote for that project was on the content and practice of those non-U.S. programs. My conclusions were that there are some initiatives outside the United States, and to varying degrees they attempt to integrate science and math, serve pre-vocational and general education purposes, cover a spectrum of engineering domains, contain basic engineering concepts, and attempt to improve the public image of engineering. In this report, I investigate standards for pre-university engineering education, also from outside the United States.

The steps in producing this report were as follows:

- First, a survey was made by Carolyn Williams (University of California) and Greg Pearson (NAE), in which they selected non-U.S. initiatives.
- This material was handed to Marc de Vries (author of this report), who added some additional initiatives from less accessible languages (German and French).
- An outline of the final report was communicated to Greg Pearson to see if the needs of the committee would be served by the proposed content.
- The author made an analytical study of what the committee could learn from the selected initiatives. The present report includes descriptions based on the Williams/Pearson survey and the additions by the author and the author's analysis.

Not surprisingly, the standards found in the preliminary survey by Carolyn Williams (University of California) and Greg Pearson (NAE) were directly related to the curriculum initiatives used in the previous project. In my own survey, I was able to add two new cases, namely from France and Germany (material that was not available in English). For some countries (Israel, Netherlands, Colombia), no standards were found in the previous report, and for that reason they are not discussed here. In this report, the focus is on the extent to which the standards in non-U.S. initiatives offer a sound basis for developing good practices for pre-university engineering education. By "sound basis," I mean that the standards are sufficiently clear and unambiguous that teachers and curriculum developers can get a clear picture of what is expected of students.

In Section 2, I describe the standards in the various initiatives. This information is partially copied from my previous report. In Section 3, I analyze the characteristics of those standards to find directions for what good standards for pre-university engineering education should look like. In this report, I do not pay much attention to the engineering content in the standards, which was the focus of my previous report. Here I focus on aspects of the forms and structure of the standards.

2. Non-U.S. Standards for Pre-University Engineering Education: Descriptions

Standards are lists of desired learning outcomes that express what students are expected to know and be able to do once they have gone through a certain educational program. Standards are not descriptions of a curriculum. One and the same set of standards can be reached by different curricula. The idea of standards is to enable social agents to develop realistic expectations of what students know and can do. In that sense, the concept of standards fits in with the ideal of quality assurance. As we will see, this general description leaves room for variations in what standards look like.

2.1 England and Wales: General Certificate of Education (GCE) in Engineering

The GCE in Engineering is one of the new A-level GCEs that have replaced the former Vocational Certificates of Education. GCEs directly precede university-level education.

In England and Wales, compulsory education runs from student ages 5 through 16 and is divided into three Key Stages: KS1 (1–3), KS2 (4–6), and KS3 (U.S. grades 7–9). England and Wales have a National Curriculum that is common for all state schools. Taken together, KS1 and KS2 are primary education, and KS3 and KS4 are secondary education. In the first three Key Stages, technology education is part of the curriculum, under the subject name Design and Technology. In these stages, the use of math and science is rather superficial, and the use of general engineering concepts is implicit, if present at all.

In the fifth year of secondary education, students take General Certificate of Secondary Education (GCSE) courses (at the Ordinary Level [O-level]), after which they can continue with Advanced Level (A-level) courses. Levels are awarded by companies, which are recognized by the government as entitled to administer the examinations and award the certificates. At this moment only one such organization, Edexcel, provides the courses and examinations for the GCE in Engineering.

At the A-level, the GCE in Engineering certificate is divided into three Advanced Subsidiaries (AS) comprising 180 guided learning hours and an A2 level, whereby AS levels are completed first and are recognized as a separate qualification. The full A-level certificate comprises AS-levels plus the A2-level. The AS-level GCE in Engineering courses were introduced in 2006, and the first full A-level certificates were awarded in 2007. In 2006, 234 of the 365 students enrolled passed the exam.

The Qualifications and Curriculum Authority (QCA) has produced "subject criteria" for the GCE in Engineering exam; the criteria "are intended to help ensure consistent and comparable standards in qualifications in the same subject/sector." This quote from the QCA document shows that subject criteria may not be exactly the same as standards, but they come close to standards because they try to give a clear picture of the qualities students will have. For illustration, the first four subject criteria are included below.

Area of study	Amplification (should normally include)
1 Legislation and documentation in engineering	Understand the importance of engineering documents, contracts, legislation and risk assessment, including: • current statutory health and safety legislation including assessment and the identification of hazards in engineering activities • industry sector standards • employment rights and responsibilities.
2 Understanding the role of engineers	Investigate/understand the role of engineers in different engineering sectors and the tasks involved in a range of engineering disciplines, including: • characteristics and roles required for successful project completion in a range of industries and sectors in which engineering plays a role.
3 The impact of engineers and engineering on society and the environment	Investigate the role that engineers and engineering play in designing and creating a modern global society and the impact they have upon it and the environment, including: • the production of manufactured goods • energy production, ie electricity, gas, coal, nuclear and petrochemicals, and renewable energy sources • food production • transport • service industries • current environmental legislation, including measures that can be taken to minimise the social and environmental impact engineering activities • reduction of waste by the efficient use of resources.
4 The application of technology in engineering	Investigate how the development of technology impacts upon engineering, including: • CAD/CAM • use of software applications • control systems • communications.

Table 1   The First Four QCA Standards

The QCA standards are grouped in 12 Areas of Study, out of which a number are selected, depending on the level (AS, AS2, or A-level). One standard is provided for each level. The terminology used is limited to "understand," "investigate," "select," "read," "evaluate," "apply," and "identify." Note that the often-used word "understand" is not very operational, that is, it does not provide clues as to how to assess it. "Understanding" is an inner or tacit quality of a person that must somehow be made external.

The subject criteria are elaborated in the syllabi produced by the commercial providers of exam materials, such as the Assessment and Qualifications Alliance (AQA). In the AQA materials, we find tables titled "Assessment Evidence," which describe actions candidates must be able to perform ("At this level candidates have . . ."). This resembles what are called standards in the United States. All of these actions are described for three "bands" that show increasing levels of competence. In general, verbs are used to indicate actions that candidates should be able to perform. Although the AQA material does not exactly follow the 12 Areas of Study in the QCA document, there is a close resemblance.

In the Edexcel material, we find another list of areas of study, here called "units": Engineering Materials, Processes and Techniques; The Role of the Engineer; Principles of Design, Planning and Prototyping; and Applied Engineering Systems. Similar to the AQA, Edexcel also provides tables with "assessment criteria" arranged in three bands, or levels. In the language, we find both verbs and products (e.g., "a plan for production"). However, it is not always clear what is expected (come up with such a plan or only be able to interpret it, etc.).

2.2 Australia

In my previous report I described the Higher School Certificate in Engineering Studies in the state of New South Wales. In this report I present information from other states as well.

One of the six Australian states, namely the state of New South Wales, offers a Higher School Certificate in Engineering Studies, similar to the British GCE in Engineering. Other states offer similar certificates, such as Engineering Studies (Western Australia), Engineering Technology (Queensland), and Systems Engineering (Victoria). The certificate in New South Wales is offered to students in grades 11 and 12 in the Australian system, usually referred to as senior secondary education (comparable to grades 11 and 12 in the United States). Education in New South Wales includes kindergarten (grade K), primary education (grades 1–6), and secondary education (grades 7–12). In some states the split between primary and secondary education is after grade 7.

As in the United States, some aspects of education are arranged at the national level and some at the state level. The inclusion of technology education as a compulsory learning area in all schools has been determined at the national level. Like the U.K., Australia has a National Curriculum that includes VET (vocational education and training) certificates that can be earned simultaneously with the general Senior Secondary Certificate.

The state of New South Wales has decided to offer a VET Certificate in Engineering Studies. In 2000, the course was revised and renamed Engineering Studies (previously it was Engineering Sciences). The New South Wales Certificate in Engineering Studies requires an understanding of the nature and practice of engineering. Students also learn basic engineering concepts, the social dimensions of engineering, and problem solving skills through a modular approach. Preliminary modules, which deal with systems that are familiar to students, such as household appliances, landscape products, braking systems, and simple biotechnology, take about 120 hours of study. Another 120 hours of more advanced modules are required to complete the certificate. These modules include civil structures, transport, lifting devices, aeronautics, and telecommunications. There is also room in the course of study for special modules of local interest.

In 2006, 1,419 students (mostly female) were enrolled in the VET Certificate in Engineering Studies program. At this time, there are no data indicating the success of the new certificate program. The former Engineering Studies Certificate resulted in 41 percent of students continuing to university, with approximately 32 percent of them pursuing science and engineering disciplines. Forty-one percent is a good score compared to the overall percentage (35 percent) of grade 12 students who continue to university.

Our research turned up standards for three Australian states—Western Australia, New South Wales, and Victoria. In all three, the list of Course Standards (Western Australia), Objectives and Outcomes (New South Wales), and Unit Titles (Victoria) are very condensed. The Western Australia materials have standards for six levels (levels 3–8). Although no indication is given of what the numbers stand for, we can assume they refer to grade levels in secondary education. The sentences describing each outcome are broken up into fragments, and the parallel printing of these fragments suggests that progression can be found in successive fragments. For instance, the second fragment continues the verb in the outcome, and the fourth fragment contains a resource used in the action expressed by the verb (see Table 2 for illustrations).

Level 3	Level 4	Level 5	Level 6	Level 7	Level 8
Students implement given	Students implement plans,	Students work cooperatively	Students work	Students proactively make	Students autonomously
plans, safely operate	safely operate equipment,	to implement plans,	collaboratively, adhere to	decisions, adhere to OH&S	make decisions, predict
equipment when using	when using traditional	recognise hazards to safely	OH&S standards, manage	regulations to minimise risk,	potential hazards at defined
traditional materials,	materials, simple techniques	operate equipment when	resources and techniques	select resources and	points, organise resources
fundamental techniques and	and technologies, and apply	using traditional materials,	efficiently, and manipulate	techniques to manage	and skills to manage
technologies, and apply	stated arithmetic formula to	techniques and	three variable formulas to	contingencies, and	contingencies, and
simple arithmetic skills to	achieve solutions to a limited	technologies, and apply	resolve predictable	manipulate multiple variable	manipulate multiple variable
achieve solutions to a set	range of predictable	dimensional arithmetic skills	challenges that meet given	equations to resolve	formulae in staged
challenge.	challenges.	to achieve solutions to a range of predictable challenges.	tolerances or performance standards.	challenges that meet precise tolerances or performance standards.	calculations to resolve diverse challenges that meet industry and commercial standards.

Table 2   A Sample of Standards in Western Australia

The same can be seen in the New South Wales document. The Victoria document, which is even more condensed, has only a few words per unit; the description can be as short as "Use hand tools" (see Table 3 for illustration).

Unit	Field of Education Code	Unit Titles	Pre-requisites	Hours
MEM 1 .2FA*	030707	Apply principles of Occupational Health & Safety in work environment.	none	20
MEM 18.1AB*	030707	Use hand tools.	none	20
MEM 1 8.2AA*	030707	Use power tools/hand held operation.	none	20
VBN768*	030799	Develop an individual career plan for the engineering industry.	none	20
VBN769*	030707	Perform basic machining processes.	none	40
VBN77O*	030101	Apply basic fabrication techniques.	none	40
VBN771*	031399	Apply electrotechnology principles in an engineering work environment.	none	20
VBN772*	030799	Use computers for engineering related work activities.	none	20
VBN773*	030701	Produce basic engineering sketches and drawings.	none	20
VBN774*	030799	Perform basic computational principles in engineering work activities.	none	20
VBN776	030101	Use basic engineering concepts to plan the manufacture of engineering components.	none	20
VBN777	030799	Handle engineering materials.	none	20
VBN778	030101	Produce basic engineering components and products using fabrication and machining.	VBN769 VBN77O VBN773	60
Core hours				340

Table 3   A Sample of Standards Used in Victoria

2.3 South Africa: Further Education and Training

In South Africa, grades 10 through 12 are called Further Education and Training (FET). Grades 1 through 9 are called General Education and Training (GET), and the first year of schooling is called a Reception Year (grade R). GET has a national curriculum and is further divided into the Foundation Phase (grades R-3), the Intermediate Phase (grades 4-6), and the Senior Phase (grades 7-9).

Since the curriculum revisions of 1998 and 2002, technology education has been a compulsory part of the GET curriculum. These revisions must be seen against the background of political changes in the country. After the abolishment of apartheid, it was necessary to ensure a good level of education for all demographic groups in the country, in particular to raise the level of education among black people. Compulsory education since the curriculum revisions is called outcomes-based education (OBE) to indicate that outcome indicators play a vital role in assessing the effectiveness of the curriculum. The outcomes are defined in terms of standards, similar to the system in the United States.

All South African education claims to be OBE, which is reflected in the Assessment Standards that have been formulated nationally. These standards are consistently phrased in terms of the behavior that is to be displayed. As in the U.K., there are three levels, one for each grade in higher secondary education. Some interesting features in these levels are four groups of "learning outcomes" for each engineering program. In my previous report, information was only available for the Electrical Engineering course, but I can now present information about four engineering courses—Civil Engineering, Electrical Technology, Mechanical Technology, and Engineering Graphics and Design. The learning outcomes are:

1. Technology, society and the environment
2. Technological process
3. Knowledge and understanding
4. Application of knowledge

For some of these outcomes, particularly for the process outcomes, there is no progression from one grade to the next. This is justified in the document because "the progress is in the degree of complexity of the content/contexts (of the process)." No further explanation is given, nor does the description of the content/contexts provide any clues as to what this means.

Another interesting feature is that a separation is made between standards and content/contexts. For each engineering domain, there is a list of standards for each of the four learning outcomes and a list of content/contexts for the same four groups. Like the standards, the content/contexts are generally described in behavioral terms ("understand," "evaluate," make," etc.). If there is no progression in the levels in the content/contexts, the same justification is given—the progression is in the degree of complexity of the content in the Learning Outcomes (see Table 4 for a sample). In the analysis in Section 3 of this report, I will show that the nature of these content/contexts is not unproblematic.

Grade 10	Grade 11	Grade 12
The content and contexts could include:		
10.1.1 understanding of the issues of environmental technology	11.1.1 describing of environmental technology	12.1.1 applying of the principles of conservation related to environmental technology
10.1.2 understanding human rights as captured in the Bill of Rights	11.1.2 discussing human rights including fairness, equality and inclusivity	12.1.2 applying human rights and work ethics
10.1.3 responding to basic medical emergencies in context, taking cognisance of health issues such as HIV/AIDS	11.1.3 responding to basic medical emergencies in context, taking cognisance of health issues such as HIV/AIDS	12.1.3 responding to basic medical emergencies in context, taking cognisance of health issues such as HIV/AIDS
10.1.4 understanding indigenous knowledge systems of different cultures	11.1.4 comparing how different cultures solve technological problems	12.1.4 analysing of solutions to technological problems in different cultures
10.1.5 understanding the principles of entrepreneurial activity	11.1.5 discussing entrepreneurial principles to help improve the economy	12.1.5 investigating entrepreneurial opportunities

Table 4   A Sample of the South African Civil Technology "Content and Contexts for the Attainment of Assessment Standards"

2.4 France

The French educational system is an interesting case study because it is much more elitist than the others. In the French system, the road to academic engineering study is preceded by a progressive selections. Clearly, the emphasis is not on trying to get more people to understand what engineering is but to get the very best students to become engineers. Pre-university engineering education is prominent in the French system, including in general education, but the pre-university education is characterized by selectivity.

Formal education in France starts with three years of kindergarten (école maternelle), followed by five years of primary school (école élémentaire) and four years of junior secondary education (collège). In collège, there is a subject analogous to technology education in U.S. junior high schools. The final four years of secondary education prepare students for the baccalauréat (known as the bac), the degree that gives entrance to tertiary education. The bac is comparable to the A-level degree in the U.K. and the Higher School Certificate in Australia.

Since 1992, there have been three types of baccalauréat—a general, a professional, and a technological baccalauréat. The general and technological baccalauréat have a common first year in which students are given an orientation that helps them choose between continuing toward the general bac or working toward the technological bac. Within the general baccalauréat, there is a scientific stream (série scientifique) that focuses on the natural sciences but has variants that focus on engineering (e.g., the série scientifique sciences de l'ingénieur).

In the baccalauréat technologique, there is a variant called the série sciences et technologies industrielles, which is currently in a process of renewal. The purpose of the renovation is both to make the content more up-to-date and to increase the number of students in academic engineering education by creating more options for studying engineering sciences after this série. In any case, students have to take a classe préparatoire aux grandes écoles (CPGE) before they can enter the grand école, where they will study engineering at university level. These classes are mainly in science and math and do not have much engineering content.

Most pupils choose the baccalauréat general. In the série scientifique the subjects in the schedule are French language, math, physics and chemistry, earth and life sciences, engineering sciences, biology/ecology, history and geography, two foreign languages, philosophy, and physical education. In the série sciences et technologies industrielles in the baccalauréat technologique, the list of subjects includes French language, history and geography, math, one foreign language, philosophy, and physical education, but also constructions, industrial systems and techniques, physics and applied physics (in the specializations of mechanical, civil, energy and materials engineering), and electronics (in the specialization electronics engineering). In terms of hours, the scientific and engineering subjects take up a substantial part of the schedule.

The Ministry of Education provides standards for the pre-university engineering education described above. The standards include an extensive list of acquired capabilities (compétences attendues) for the themes of Functional Analysis of Products, Technological Solutions Associated with Functions, Introduction to State and Behavior of Systems, and Realizing a Mini-project. For each subtheme there is also a list of knowledges (savoirs), related to the capabilities, which are distributed over four levels. No effort is made to indicate progress within a capability or knowledge. There are only different capabilities for different levels (see Table 5 for a sample of standards).

COMPÉTENCES ATTENDUES	SAVOIRS ET SAVOIR-FAIRE ASSOCIÉS	NIVEAU D'ACQUISITION			
		1	2	3	4
▪ Identifier les éléments transformés par le produit. ▪ Décrire la valeur ajoutée apportée par le produit et énoncer sa fonction de base.	1.1 Expression du besoin – Marché, client, concurrence. – Coûts, rapport qualité-prix. – Satisfaction du besoin, notion de valeur d'usage.	X X X			
▪ Configurer, régler le produit dans des cas simples et le faire fonctionner dans un mode de fonctionnement normal. ▪ Distinguer la fonction de base parmi les fonctions de service : une fonction d'usage d'une fonction d'estime ; une fonction de service d'une fonction technique. ▪ Repérer les solutions constructives associées aux fonctions techniques qui contribuent à la réalisation des fonctions d'usage.	1.2 Produit et valeur ajoutée – Frontière d'un produit technique. – Interacteurs. – Fonctions de service et fonction de base d'un produit. – Nature des éléments transformés par le produit : matières, énergies, informations. – Caractéristiques d'entrée et de sortie des éléments transformés.		X X X X X		
	1.3 Organisation fonctionnelle des produits – Fonctions d'usage. – Contraintes. – Fonctions techniques associées. – Chaîne de fonctions : - chaîne d'énergie, - chaîne d'information.		X X X X		
	1.4 Outils d'expression de l'analyse fonctionnelle – Diagramme de décomposiion fonctionnelle de type « pourquoi ? comment ? » (FAST). – Autres représentations graphiques des systèmes (diagramme d'activité, synoptique, schéma-bloc).	X	X		

Table 5   Sample of French Standards

2.5 Germany

As in Australia and the United States, German education is determined both nationally and by the states. Each German state (Länd) is authorized to determine the content of the curriculum, but the types of schools are defined at the national level. Primary education covers grades 1-4 or 1-6, depending on the state. Technology education is sometimes part of the curriculum, although this is the exception rather than the rule. In secondary education, there are different school types, representing different (cognitive) levels. The status of technology education, as well as the extent to which it deals with engineering content, differs widely. In some states it is a separate compulsory subject, in some it is part of a wider subject, often called work education, and in some it is taught only in cross-disciplinary projects.

The city of Hamburg has a document that contains the senior secondary exam for technology (Abiturprufung Technik); however, no document was found for the state of which Hamburg is the capital. The document lists three domains of accomplishments (Anforderungsbereiche) numbered I, II and III. In my analysis in Section 3, I will show the nature of these levels, each of which is subdivided into content-related knowledge and skills and process-related knowledge and skills. Most of these are described in behavioral language. The document also includes a list of Operators: general skills for engineering, such as "name," "describe," "realize," "measure," "estimate," "develop," design," "choose," "optimize," and so on.

A second example comes from Thuringia, which has a special type of vocational school (berufliches Gymnasium) for which there is a variant specialization in technology (Technik). The standards document we have contains aims (Lernziele) for only three domains: information systems, programming, and operating systems. Thus pre-engineering education here is limited to IT (see Table 6 for a sample).

Lerngebiet: Programmierung

Lerninhalte	Der Schüler kann
Nutzung einer visuellen Entwicklungsumgebung zum Erstellen objekt-orientierter Programme.	– mindestens eine moderne, objektorientierte Programmiersprache sachgerecht anwenden – ereignisorientierte Lösungsalgorithmen und softwareergonomische Benutzeroberflächen entwickeln
Klassenentwicklung	– komplexere technische und wirtschaftliche Abläufe analysieren und diese durch Modellierungstechniken in Klassen- und Objektstrukturen überführen
UML-Modellierung	– Sprachunabhängige UML-Strukturierungselemente einsetzen

Table 6 Sample of the Standards in Thuringia

3. Analysis
Some themes for analysis emerge from the description of the standards documents:

- the use of behavioral and non-behavioral terms
- levels within or among capabilities and knowledge elements
- differences in the level of detail in descriptions of standards
- differences among standards in terms of capabilities and content/contexts in which these capabilities are to be applied and the mixture of capabilities and content elements in standards descriptions

We will now examine these in more detail and compare standards documents.

3.1 Behavioral and Non-behavioral Terms
In this analysis I refer to behavioral terms as terms that contain verbs that signify visible actions, such as *explain*, *use*, etc. Non-behavioral terms are terms that contain verbs that signify internal qualities that must be externalized to be assessed (e.g., *understand* and *know*).

The material from South Africa particularly raises the issues of whether standards should be completely expressed in terms of observable behavior or if, perhaps, certain learning outcomes can only be described as internal qualities that are not directly visible. The South African standards are explicitly based on the conviction that every standard must be assessable by means of the behavior that demonstrates that knowledge or a capability has indeed been mastered. This is expressed in the term outcomes-based education (OBE), which is a key term in the South African curriculum documents.

The OBE approach is apparent in the headings of all standards listings. Let us take, for example, Learning Outcomes 1 in the Civil Engineering Standards: Technology, Society and the Environment. The Table of Standards is preceded by the following sentence: "The learner is able to *demonstrate* (my italics) an awareness and understanding of the interrelationship between Technology, society and the environment." The table itself is headed by the words: "We know this when the learner is able to:" and then, in the table, we find words such as "describe," "explain," "discuss," "predict," "respond to," "identify," "compare," "analyze," and "evaluate." All of these terms are behavioral in nature. Even though the standard itself expresses an internal quality of the learner, such as knowing or understanding, the qualities are consistently expressed in behavioral terms.

We find this approach throughout the list following Learning Outcomes 2. The Technological Process; Learning Outcomes 3. Knowledge and Understanding; and Learning Outcomes 4. Application of Knowledge. The Standards for Electrical Technology are divided into the same four Learning Outcomes. The exact content of these, of course, is different from the Civil Engineering Outcomes, but we find the same behavioral terms, "describe," "identify," and so on. The same holds true for the third program, Mechanical Technologies, and the fourth program, Engineering Graphics and Design.

The consistency with which the South African standards have been formulated in behavioral terms is even more striking when compared to standards in the other non-U.S. countries in this study. The standards in Hamburg, Germany, are probably the closest to the South African OBE approach. The Hamburg standards are interesting because they include a wide variety of behavioral terms, which even serve as an ordering principle for the standards; the standards are arranged in a table with these headings: "name," "arrange," "describe," "realize," "explain," "solve," "measure," "sketch," "draw," "calculate," "evaluate," "estimate," "relate," "design," "construct," "develop," "test," "optimize," and "choose." These terms are not atypical for Germany, as we can see by comparing the Hamburg and Thuringia standards (for information technology). However, in Thuringia they are not used as a principle for arranging all of the standards, as they are in the Hamburg materials.

In the Australian standards, too, we see a strong preference for behavioral terms, "use," "investigate," "optimize," "manage," and so on. But in the Australian materials, not all of the terms are behavioral. Many standards are expressed in terms of "understand" and "recognize," which are considerably less behavior-oriented than the terms in the South African materials.

The UK standards, as formulated by the QCA, have an even stronger bias toward the term "understand," although we also find the terms "investigate," "select," "read," "interpret," and "generate," which are of a more behavioral type. In the elaboration by the commercial assessment bodies we again find more behavioral terms. In the AQA materials we find, for instance, a Unit on Design and Graphical Communication (for the A2). The table containing the standards is headed by the words: "At this level all candidates have:" followed by "produced," "generated," "demonstrated," "explained," and the like. The same holds true for other units, such as Engineered Products and Application of Technology. In the Edexcel materials (Award-level), we find different unit names (1. Engineering Materials, Processes and Techniques; 2. The Role of the Engineer; 3. Principles of Design, Planning and Prototyping; 4. Applied Engineering

Systems; 5. The Engineering Environment; and 6. Applied Design, Planning and Prototyping), but the same types of behavioral expressions in the standards (e.g., the word "identifies" appears frequently).

The French standards are structured in a different way and allow for substantial non-behavioral terminology. All standards are divided into "competences" and "knowledge and related knowledge" (the latter probably refers to knowledge related to certain competences). Here we are quite far removed from the OBE approach.

Thus, we have seen a spectrum from a strong dominance of behavioral terms to equal space for behavioral and non-behavioral terms. An interesting question, of course, is whether standards ought to be formulated exclusively in a behavioral way or if non-behavioral standards can make equal sense. Clearly, behavioral terms have the advantage of allowing for assessment in terms of observable phenomena (e.g., if a standards says that a student is able to use a hammer, then having the student perform this is a direct way of assessing whether or not this is true), although some behavioral terms are more problematic than others. How can one "see" if a learner "knows" something?

On the other hand, some caution about excluding non-behavioral standards may be healthy. Is it really possible to express everything a learner has learned in terms of behavior? The philosophy of technology has shown that some of what engineers know is "tacit" knowledge and is very difficult to externalize (see, for instance, chapter 3 in my book, *Teaching About Technology*, Springer, 2005). A second argument against the exclusion of non-behavioral standards is that attitude theorists (e.g., Fishbein and Ajzen, *Belief, Attitude, Intention and Behavior*, Addison-Wesley, 1975) have always emphasized that the relationship between attitudes as an internal quality of people and actual behavior is indirect, at best. Does this mean that attitudinal standards should be banned because they cannot be assessed well by observing behavior? Probably not, even though this still leaves open the question of how to assess such standards properly.

3.2 The Use of Levels in Standards

Another distinguishing feature in non-U.S. standards is the use of levels. We find levels also in U.S. Standards for Technological Literacy, for which all 20 standards have been elaborated for grade levels K-2, 3-5, 6-8, and 9-12. In the U.S. standards, levels are used to indicate the degree of mastery through the various grade levels. However, indicating progression through levels of standards is certainly not easy, as we see when we look at various standards in non-U.S. countries. Some countries evidently have abstained from defining levels at all, and some countries use levels not to indicate progression but to indicate the level of required mastery for each individual standard.

In theory, one can think of several options for indicating progression through levels, some of which are:

- from concrete to abstract
- from simple to complex
- from little to more of the same
- the addition of new elements for each level

We will investigate the options used in the non-U.S. standards in this study.

The QCA materials in the U.K. do not distinguish between levels, but this can be explained because the standards indicate only the final exam level. The AQA and the Edexcel materials do distinguish between levels, apparently to indicate intermediate levels of mastery. These levels are meant to indicate progression. The AQA Standards have three levels (Bands). Terminology for the lower levels (simple, basic, limited range) indicates that the "from simple to complex" option is strongly featured here. The levels are not used for all units; for example, no levels are defined for Unit 3, Application of Technology.

The Edexcel materials also use levels for only three of four units. Here we see added verbs for each next level (e.g., "identifies" for Band 1, and "identifies and explains" for higher levels). We also recognize the same sort of indications of progression as in the AQA materials. In many cases, the progression is not indicated for each next level in the Edexcel materials, but only for the transition from Band 2 to Band 3, whereas in the AQA materials the level descriptions were different for nearly all levels and standards.

Of the Australian standards, only the standards for the Certificate of Education in Western Australia has levels (3-8, which probably refer to grade levels). In several cases, new verbs added for each next level indicate progression. For instance, in Outcome 1 (Engineering Process), the first standard has "investigate" for level 5, "investigate and justify" for level 6, and "investigate, analyze and justify" for level 7. This is an example of "adding new elements for each next level."

Another standard, "graphical representations" for level 4 and "a range of graphical representations" for level 5, illustrates the principle of "from little to more of the same." We also find the "from concrete to abstract" and "from simple to complex" approaches. For instance, one standard has in level 8 "understand integrated complex multiple staged scientific principles and mathematical relationships underpinning conservation of energy," while in all lower levels the word "complex" does not appear; the "scientific principles and mathematical relationships" are present only in level 6 and up. Several standards have combinations of the four options for progression, which makes it difficult to characterize the overall progression in these standards. There is no common pattern for the whole set of standards for Western Australia.

The South African standards show the same use of multiple types of levels for standards. For each of standard, the requirement is indicated for grades 10, 11, and 12. It is striking, though, that the South African materials have no progression for Learning Outcome 2. Technological Process. The standard document states: "The progression across the grades is reflected in the degree of complexity of the content in Learning Outcomes 3 and 4." But those are Knowledge and Understanding and Application of Knowledge, so evidently no progression is defined for the process in which the knowledge is learned and/or used. Looking at the whole set of South African standards, one soon finds that no attempt has been made to formulate progression for some of the other standards.

In the standards for which progression has been formulated, the progression is often suggested by the word "describe" for lower grades and words like "discuss," "explain," and "analyse" for higher grades. However, this is not done consistently, because in some cases we find "explain" in the lowest level also, and in some cases we find "understand" in the lowest level and "describe" in a higher level. In the Content/Contexts for the attainment of Assessment Standards, Learning Outcome 1. Technology, Society and the Environment, for instance, we find "understanding of the issues of environmental technology" for Grade 10 and "describing of environmental technology" for Grade 11. One can question what the progression is here. In general, the differences between levels are often marginal. Evidently, the South African materials are not quite clear about the use of levels for standards.

In the French Standards we find four levels. Here they are not meant to indicate progression, however. Instead, they indicate to which level each of the standards has to be mastered. Some standards only have to be mastered at level 1, others at level 2, and so on. The four levels are defined as follows: 1. Level of being informed ("knowing what one speaks about"); 2. Level of being able to express ("being able to talk about it"); 3. Level of application ("being able to do"); 4. Level of methodological mastery ("being able to choose, analyze, synthesize, and evaluate"). This reminds one vaguely of Bloom's classic taxonomy, published originally in *Handbook on Formative and Summative Evaluation of Student Learning (*McGraw-Hill, 1971). These same levels are used for all standards. Of course, the practical meaning varies among standards, and for that reason each description is preceded by a short explanation of what "niveau d'information," "niveau d'expression," "niveau des outils," and "niveau de la maîtrise méthodologique" (the four levels, as explained above) mean for that particular standard.

In the Hamburg material, the behavioral terms are to be applied in three domains (Anforderungsbereiche), which, in fact, represent levels. The first domain is reproduction of content in the context in which it was learned. The second domain is transfer of the learned content to a new context. The third domain requires that the learner choose the appropriate content for a complex problem in a different context from the one in which the content was learned. This seems to be the "from concrete to abstract" option for progression, as being able to transfer a concept from one context to another requires knowledge at a higher level of abstraction than being able to apply knowledge in a single context. Again there is some similarity with Bloom's taxonomy. The table of operators (the behavioral terms used to indicate standards) shows on which level (domain) each standard has to be mastered. Here we see a combination of using levels for indicating progression (Level II is more demanding than Level I, and Level III is more demanding than Level II) and for indicating the required level of mastery for each standard.

The U.S. Standards for Technological Literacy clearly are most akin to the South African standards, which use a combination of approaches to indicate progress. Most of the other non-U.S. standards are based on a single approach, mostly "from concrete to abstract" or "from simple to complex." With the combination of approaches, it is very difficult to consistently indicate what constitutes progression and to characterize overall progression. It may well be that in anticipation of these difficulties other countries have abstained from using more than one approach at a time to indicate progression.

3.3 Level of Detail
The non-U.S. standards in our sample differ substantially in their level of detail.

In the Hamburg materials, the description of standards is very concise—simply a list of 25 "Operators" combined with a short description of three levels. Each operator is defined in one sentence. The description of the Australian standards, too, has little detail. The Western Australia standards are described in one sentence each, and the nine standards are ordered in four "Outcomes." The New South Wales standards are even shorter: five standards with a one-sentence description of each. The twelve compulsory and seven elective Victoria standards are also described in a short sentence for each.

The French material is more elaborate and more detailed. Ten tables describe the standards, each of which is subdivided into three to six elements for the competences and seven to ten elements for related knowledge. In addition, there are four levels for each main category of standards. The U.K. material is concise in describing end-level standards (a short list of 11 standards, each of which is described in a short sentence with a few bullets to indicate elements in the standard), but the elaborations in the AQA and Edexcel materials include more detailed descriptions (each standard is elaborated for three bands, or levels).

The South African materials contain the most detailed descriptions. The materials of Civil Technology include 30 standards with different descriptions for each of the three grades and an equal number of content/contexts descriptions for the attainment of each standard.

Detailed and elaborate standards and concise, short standards both have pros and cons. Very detailed, elaborate standards leave little room for curriculum developers to put their own stamp on the material to be learned. There are so many standards that one can only decide how to arrange them in a way that makes sense to teachers and learners, but one has few choices in terms of content.

More concise descriptions offer more opportunities for different ways of elaborating the standards in different directions. However, this is only an advantage if teachers have the necessary capabilities to elaborate on them in a sophisticated way. In the past decade, the U.K. has moved back and forth between more and less detailed descriptions of its standards for "Design and Technology" education in response to the tension between the advantage of having open standards, which allows good schools to develop excellent practices, and short descriptions of standards that provide more direction for weaker schools to help them develop good practices.

3.4 Capabilities and Contexts
Recent educational theories (constructivism, concept-context approach) suggest that learning should take place in practical contexts. The theories are based on the principle that by learning in different contexts, the learner gradually develops a generic level of knowledge and skills. This contrasts with the view that concepts and capabilities can be learned independent of context and directly at an abstract level. The new approaches are reflected in some of the non-U.S. standards in our sample, in which a distinction is made between the content of what is to be learned and the contexts in which that content is to be learned and/or applied.

In two countries, a distinction is made between the capabilities to be mastered and the contexts in which they must be applied. At first glance, this seems to be what the Hamburg materials do, but as we have seen, these domains indicate levels of mastery rather than application domains. In the South African materials, however, there is a real separation between assessment standards and content and contexts for the attainment of assessment standards. The meaning of the term context, however, appears to be different from the meaning in the recent educational theories mentioned above, in which context is a social practice (e.g., taking part in traffic by going from home to school or participating in electronic communities).

Let us take a closer look at the South African Learning Outcome 1: Technology, Society and the Environment. The first standard here is: "Describe the interrelationship between technology, society and the environment" for Grade 10, "Discuss and evaluate the interrelationship between technology, society and the environment" for Grade 11, and "Predict the impact of future development in technology on society and the environment" for Grade 12. We have discussed elsewhere the nature of the progression through the grades. The content and contexts for the same standard are: "understanding of the issues of environmental technology" for Grade 10, "describing of environmental technology" for Grade 11, and "applying of the principles of conservation related to environmental technology" for Grade 12.

In this example, it is not clear at all what the differences are. Further investigation into the standards and accompanying content and contexts shows that sometimes the very same words are used in the standards themselves and the accompanying content and contexts. The only differences are that sometimes the content/contexts are slightly more specific (for instance, the principle of conservation is mentioned in the content and contexts but not in the standard itself).

Clearly, the idea of separating standards and the contexts in which they can be applied has not been worked out in the South African materials. Still, the idea is worth considering. In principle there is an advantage to making this separation. The standards themselves could then be phrased in generic terms that leave open opportunities for curriculum developers to use different, perhaps locally relevant contexts, for applications of the standards.

The very same distinction is used in a current Delphi study by Hofstra University (in collaboration with the author) aimed at identifying broad, basic concepts for engineering and technology education and contexts in which these concepts can be taught and learned. In principle, it would be interesting to use the same distinction in standards for pre-college/university engineering education. The South African materials show that more reflection on how to do this properly will be needed.

4. Conclusions

What lessons can be drawn from this survey and analysis for the work of the committee? The analysis has shown that the non-U.S. examples of standards for pre-college/university engineering education have some interesting ideas that may be worth considering, even though they have not always been well elaborated.

4.1 Lessons Learned

One of the problematic issues in formulating standards is the notion of progression through levels (e.g., in the U.S. Standards for Technological Literacy). As we have seen, of all the non-U.S. standards in the survey, the South African standards, which are the most similar to the U.S. Standards for Technological Literacy, are inconsistent in the way they define the differences between levels. Because several types of progression are mixed, it is very difficult to see what the overall progression is.

Some of the non-U.S. standards are based on a different approach that is interesting to consider. This alternative is to formulate the same levels for all standards, as is done in the Hamburg example. By relating these levels to classic taxonomies, such as Bloom's, there is at least some indication that the levels have a certain validity.

A second interesting suggestion based on non-U.S. standards is the separation of standards and the contexts in which they can be taught and learned. This separation can result in more generic standards that can be described in less detail and hence are easy to survey. This approach enables teachers to recognize more easily the essence of what is to be learned and how much freedom teachers and schools have in conveying that content. Studies like the current Delphi study by Hofstra and Delft universities can help identify the essence of what is to be learned in engineering concepts and contexts.

4.2 What Remains to Be Done

The survey shows that some puzzles have not been solved yet and need further research. In particular, the issue of "outcomes-based" or "non-outcomes-based" standards is something most developers of standards are evidently struggling with. It appears that it is difficult to be consistent in formulating all standards in behavioral terminology, and one can question if this should be aimed for at all. But then we must ask how standards formulated in a non-behavioral way can be assessed. That is still unclear. Perhaps we just have to accept that some educational goals, particularly long-term attitudinal goals, cannot be fully assessed.

A second unresolved issue is the relatively small number of examples of non-U.S. standards for pre-college/university engineering education. By selecting only initiatives that have standards, we have even fewer examples here than we had in the previous study of curricula. Some initiatives for pre-college/university engineering education outside the U.S. have material for classrooms, but these materials do not appear to be based on standards.

Clearly, there is a lack of experience everywhere in drawing up sound standards for pre-college engineering education. In many ways, the U.S. Standards for Technological Literacy are more sophisticated and elaborate than standards developed outside the United States, even though the U.S. standards are not intended solely to support engineering learning. This suggests that the United States may have the experience base to develop quality engineering education standards for grades K–12. It would make sense, however, to seek ways of developing these standards in cooperation with countries that, according to this survey, have some experience and may have gained some useful insights.

The Development of Technology/Engineering Concepts in Massachusetts Academic Standards

Jacob Foster, Director of Science and Technology/Engineering
Massachusetts Department of Elementary and Secondary Education

**Commissioned paper for the National Academy of Engineering
July 8, 2009**

Over the past decade Massachusetts has developed academic technology/engineering standards and implemented related programs. The Massachusetts experience has become a reference point for a number of other states and countries looking to support engineering education. This paper outlines the process Massachusetts has undertaken and some of the successes and challenges related to the implementation of engineering concepts in K–12 education.

The development of state technology/engineering standards was initially made possible through the Massachusetts 1993 Education Reform Law but was only carried out through the advocacy of technology education educators and engineers with an interest in education. Massachusetts treats technology/engineering as a science discipline, equivalent to physical science, life science, and earth and space science. A number of state policies support the implementation of school and district technology/engineering programs aligned with the technology/engineering standards, such as licensure and assessment expectations. A number of challenges remain, however, before technology/engineering can be considered to have developed to a point equivalent to traditional science disciplines.[2]

History of Technology/Engineering in Massachusetts

The development of technology/engineering standards in Massachusetts started with the inclusion of language in the 1993 Massachusetts Education Reform Law:

> The board shall . . . develop *academic standards* for the core subjects of mathematics, *science and technology*, history and social science, English, foreign languages and the arts. . . . The board may also include in the standards a fundamental knowledge of *technology education* and computer science and keyboarding skills. . . (Massachusetts General Laws, Chapter 69, Section 1D, italics added)

The inclusion of "science and technology" in this legislation was the impetus for the development of the first state *MA Science and Technology Framework* (MA ESE, 1996). The

---

[2] This paper focuses on academic standards and programs. The state also has Career/Vocational Technical Education (CVTE) frameworks with engineering foci, including Engineering Technology, Biotechnology, and Robotics and Automation Technology, among others. While fairly new (2007), there are a growing number of these programs in voc tech schools across the state. The CVTE frameworks can be found at: http://www.doe.mass.edu/cte/frameworks/

inclusion of the word "technology" in this label sparked a state-wide discussion of what that should include. For the science education community, it was indicative of a science, technology, and society (STS) perspective reflective of *Science for All Americans* (AAAS, 1989) and the *National Science Education Standards* (NRC, 1996). For the technology education community, it suggested a technological literacy perspective reflective of *Technology for All Americans* (ITEA, 1996). There was some discussion as to whether it meant computers—instructional technology—but the later inclusion of the label "technology education" in the statement about what the board "may also include" was interpreted as a reference to computers.

The result of this state-wide discussion was an initial (1996) state framework that defined "science and technology" as an academic subject that integrated the STS and technology education perspectives. Later, in the 2001 framework revision (MA ESE, 2001), the STS perspective was reduced and replaced with more specific engineering principles, leading to the modified framework title "science and technology/engineering."

The Vision of Technology/Engineering

This paper is not the place to outline the reasons technology/engineering education adds significant value to student learning and to our educational programs. Those rationales have been well developed elsewhere. However, it is worth explaining the general motivations of those who advocated for technology/engineering in Massachusetts during each stage of the framework process.

During the development of the initial 1996 framework, technology education staff promoted the need for students to develop technological literacy in addition to scientific literacy. They also strongly argued that technology education courses promoted hands-on opportunities for students, particularly a certain population of students who were not succeeding in "traditional" science courses. These arguments spelled out the educational value of the discipline.

A third argument was related to adults rather than students. Advocates for this arguments noted that including technology education in a core academic framework would justify their jobs. It was their contention that administrators would find it harder to eliminate technology education programs if those programs directly contributed to student learning of a core academic discipline.

In the revision process leading to the 2001 framework, engineers with an interest in education entered the conversation to advocate for expanding the technology component of the framework to include engineering principles. These engineers argued that standards would be necessary to promote engaging, innovative programs to interest students in current methods and issues of design and support the state's need for engineers and technicians.

The Academic Framework over Time

Basic Structure

The state science standards follow a consistent format: strands (disciplines) include a number of core topics that are specified through standards. There are five strands in the current MA framework: Earth and Space Science, Life Science (Biology at the high school level), Physical

Science (splits into Chemistry and Introductory Physics at the high school level), and Technology/Engineering. The strands are treated equally in state policies, such as course credit for graduation, licensure, and state testing. Each strand is made up of 6 to 9 topics; each topic has 2 to10 standards.

Influential Reference Documents
The development of the initial *1996 MA Science and Technology Curriculum Framework* drew upon the nation's seminal standards documents for science education, including the *National Science Education Standards* (NRC, 1996) and the *Benchmarks for Scientific Literacy* (AAAS, 1993), as well as the *1996 NAEP Science Framework* (USED, 1996). For the *2001 MA Science and Technology/Engineering Curriculum Framework*, the NRC and AAAS documents were once again used as references with the *2000 NAEP Science Framework* (USED, 2000) and *Standards for Technological Literacy* (ITEA, 2000) added as core references. In addition, policy factors the led to the articulation of the 2001 No Child Left Behind Act (NCLB) were considered, specifically the expectation that content would be a central focus.

For the expected 2011 revision of the framework, the seminal science and technology education documents are again being used as references, substituting the *2009 NAEP Science Framework* (USED, 2008) and adding references being developed by Achieve, Inc., that analyze international benchmarks.

1996 Framework Technology Topics and Sample Standards
With references and advocacy from both the science and technology education communities, the technology topics in the initial 1996 framework reflect the combined STS and technology education perspectives:

1996 Technology Topics (high school)
- The design process
- The nature and impact of technology
- Technology yesterday, today, and tomorrow
- The tools and machines of technology
- Resources of technology
- Technological areas of communication, construction, manufacturing, transportation, power, and bio-related technologies

---

Figure 1 High school technology topics in the 1996 MA Science and Technology Curriculum Framework.

These combined perspectives are also found in the specific standards:

Resources of Technology
* Identify particular characteristics of material resources, i.e., synthetic, composite, and biological. Explain how various energy sources and forms of information are also resources with specific characteristics.
* Discuss issues of resource management including safety, costs, environmental and political concerns. Discuss a current example such as waste management and nuclear power systems.

Technological Areas of Communication, Construction, Manufacturing, Transportation, Power, and Bio-related Technologies
* Give examples of how combinations of graphic and electronic communication processes are used in developing high technology communication systems.
* Describe uses of material conversion processes, i.e., separating, forming, conditioning and combining, in production processes.
* Identify ways that manufacturing processes have changed with improved tools and techniques.
* Compare how existing transportation technologies convey people and products globally.
* Give examples of ways in which technological processes could adversely affect the environment. Choose a current example from your local news to investigate.

Figure 2 Sample 1996 standards for two technology topics.

2001 Framework Technology/Engineering Topics and Sample Standards

With the advocacy of engineers interested in education, a number of changes were made to the technology topics and standards in the framework. Specifically, technological design was modified to become the engineering design process, additional topics for energy and power systems were added, and the social implications of technology were removed. The technology/engineering topics found in the 2001 framework reflect the combined technology education and engineering perspectives:

2001 Technology/Engineering Topics (high school)
* Engineering design
* Materials, tools, and machines
* Communication technologies
* Manufacturing technologies
* Construction technologies
* Transportation technologies
* Energy and power systems—fluid systems
* Energy and power systems—thermal systems
* Energy and power systems—electrical systems
* Bioengineering technologies

Figure 3 High school technology/engineering topics in the 2001 MA Science and Technology/Engineering Curriculum Framework.

These perspectives are also reflected in the specific standards:

---

2. Construction Technologies

Central Concepts: The construction process is a series of actions taken to build a structure, including preparing a site, setting a foundation, erecting a structure, installing utilities, and finishing a site. Various materials, processes, and systems are used to build structures. Students should demonstrate and apply the concepts of construction technology through building and constructing either full-size models or scale models using various materials commonly used in construction. Students should demonstrate the ability to use the engineering design process to solve a problem or meet a challenge in construction technology.

2.1 Identify and explain the engineering properties of materials used in structures (e.g., elasticity, plasticity, R value, density, strength).

2.2 Distinguish among tension, compression, shear, and torsion, and explain how they relate to the selection of materials in structures.

2.3 Explain Bernoulli's principle and its effect on structures such as buildings and bridges.

2.4 Calculate the resultant force(s) for a combination of live loads and dead loads.

2.5 Identify and demonstrate the safe and proper use of common hand tools, power tools, and measurement devices used in construction.

2.6 Recognize the purposes of zoning laws and building codes in the design and use of structures.

3. Energy and Power Technologies—Fluid Systems

Central Concepts: Fluid systems are made up of liquids or gases and allow force to be transferred from one location to another. They can also provide water, gas, and/or oil, and/or remove waste. They can be moving or stationary and have associated pressures and velocities. Students should demonstrate the ability to use the engineering design process to solve a problem or meet a challenge in a fluid system.

3.1 Explain the basic differences between open fluid systems (e.g., irrigation, forced hot air system, air compressors) and closed fluid systems (e.g., forced hot water system, hydraulic brakes).

3.2 Explain the differences and similarities between hydraulic and pneumatic systems, and explain how each relates to manufacturing and transportation systems.

3.3 Calculate and describe the ability of a hydraulic system to multiply distance, multiply force, and effect directional change.

3.4 Recognize that the velocity of a liquid moving in a pipe varies inversely with changes in the cross-sectional area of the pipe.

3.5 Identify and explain sources of resistance (e.g., 45° elbow, 90° elbow, changes in diameter) for water moving through a pipe.

Figure 4 Sample 2001 central concepts and standards for two technology/engineering topics.

Emergence of Academic Technology/Engineering in Massachusetts

The incorporation of technology/engineering standards into the core academic framework, initially led by the state technology education organization, was a first step toward incorporating these concepts into the educational system. In the early to mid 1990s, industrial arts made a shift to technology education. The technology education programs at the time (many of which still exist) are generally characterized as elective, supplementary programs that focus primarily on the development of student skills and products, but not on trade skills or tool use as industrial arts had emphasized. The new discussion about becoming a core academic discipline pushed technology education to consider the implications of yet another shift: moving away from a supplemental, technical-oriented technology education program toward an academic, knowledge-oriented technology/engineering program.

This change was even further removed from the long and productive history of skills development and tool use. Although individual teachers made progress in making this transition, and created an initial set of technology/engineering courses in the process, many technology education staff did not want to make another shift. Thus the implications of the second shift continue to pose a significant challenge to the systematic implementation of technology/engineering standards in Massachusetts.

The question has split the state's technology education organization in two: one side is aligned more with the industrial arts/technology education perspective and the other is aligned with the technology/engineering-academic perspective. People watching this process, including school and district science staff, curriculum coordinators, and administrators, took the split as one reason to delay the incorporation of technology/engineering concepts into school programs.

Between 1996 and the mid-2000s, science staff and organizations generally did not take ownership of technology/engineering standards, which they viewed as the responsibility of technology education teachers. Another reason for delay, not associated with the organizational events but related to the recent shift away from industrial arts, was that educational staff and parents were slow to change their conception of past technical-oriented programs and embrace the possibility of an academic technology/engineering program.

Only recently have more schools and districts begun to transition technology education programs into their science departments. Those that have often merge the two departments into a "science and technology/engineering department." This is due, in part, to several developments. First, the MA Department of Elementary and Secondary Education (the Department) has worked over the years to align all state policies so that technology/engineering is treated the same way all other science disciplines are treated. This provides schools and districts with the support they need to develop academic technology/engineering programs. Second, relationships between the two technology education organizations are starting to heal. And finally, the Boston Museum of Science (the Museum), with its associated National Center for Technological Literacy, has become a leader in promoting technology/engineering.

These developments have moved the discipline away from the tensions of organizational strife and associations with past technical programs. The Museum's development of technology/engineering curriculum provided an image for administrators, science staff, and parents of what a technology/engineering curriculum could look like. It also showed how technology/engineering concepts were related to more traditional science concepts. In addition to educating administrators and guidance staff, the curriculum has had a significant impact on the establishment of technology/engineering programs across the state.[3]

---

[3] The National Center for Technological Literacy (NCTL) at the Boston Museum of Science has trained over 750 teachers in the Engineering is Elementary (EiE) curriculum across Massachusetts, where approximately 115 elementary schools are now using EiE. Approximately 60 high schools have purchased the Engineering the Future (EtF) curriculum. Many high school teachers have participated in training for the EtF curriculum as well (numbers

Development of Department Policies

Policy Successes

Although it has taken years, significant progress has been made by the Department in aligning the various policy elements so that technology/engineering is now treated as an academic discipline. The grounding in the state's 1993 Education Reform Law was essential for making this possible. The law not only provided a basis for developing the standards, it also provided the justification for developing corresponding policies.

The Department has repeatedly pointed out similarities between the structures of technology/engineering and traditional sciences. Both articulate a core body of knowledge, and both have an articulated process (closely aligned) to guide practice and generate new knowledge. Based on these "equivalences," the Department has claimed (from a policy perspective) that technology/engineering can be counted *as a science.* This rationale supports changes to all other policy elements

Once the first framework was developed, changes to the state's science assessment followed. Since technology/engineering was recognized as a strand in the framework, equivalent to other science disciplines, the Massachusetts Comprehensive Assessment System (MCAS) incorporated technology/engineering items into its assessment. Technology/engineering currently counts for 15 percent of the grade 5 test and 25 percent of the grade 8 test and is one of four options for the high school end-of-course test.

Next, the licensure expectations for teachers of technology/engineering had to be adjusted. This took much longer to implement. The Department currently offers an academic "technology/engineering" license which has expectations equivalent to those of other science licenses: required content knowledge (including passing a content test), completion of a practicum, available licenses for grade PreK–8 and 5–12, and being "highly qualified" as required by NCLB.

However, because technology/engineering evolved through the progression of industrial arts to technology education to technology/engineering, the license was not completely new; it is actually a transition of the corresponding licenses of the same titles. As a result, all industrial arts and technology education certified teachers have been grandfathered into the system with licenses to teach a core academic technology/engineering course. This arrangement provided a pool of teachers qualified to teach the new subject, but it also led to confusion by administrators about whether those teachers were *really* qualified.

Finally, since the state recognizes technology/engineering as a core academic science option, schools and districts can award science credit for these courses and apply them to high school graduation requirements. The alignment of all of these policies means that schools and districts now have the support they need to develop academic technology/engineering programs.

---

are not currently available). In addition, NCTL has supported leadership teams in approximately 55 Massachusetts districts, including over 250 teachers and administrators, to design and implement technology/engineering programs.

Policy Challenge

The one significant remaining policy challenge is to align high school graduation expectations and state college admission requirements. This issue has only recently come to the fore because it has taken until now for technology/engineering programs to produce a significant number of students with these credits. Second, addressing the issue requires alignment between the Department, the Massachusetts Department of Higher Education, and, interestingly, the National Collegiate Athletic Association (NCAA).

Although the Department allows schools to apply technology/engineering courses to science graduation requirements, the Department of Higher Education does not yet recognize those courses as "natural/physical science" courses for the purposes of college admission. Since most higher education institutions have separate science and engineering departments, these disciplines are not immediately considered equivalent. Added to that, institutions of higher education have not had a chance to assess the nature or rigor of high school technology/engineering courses. Thus when they conduct a transcript review for purposes of student admission, technology/engineering courses are not being counted as fulfilling science requirements. This issue is being actively addressed and will hopefully be resolved before long.

Alignment with NCAA requirements is a bit more abstract but just as important. NCAA conducts its own transcript reviews of students who want to play or receive sports scholarships at NCAA-affiliated institutions. NCAA reviews the high school syllabus (submitted to NCAA by high school guidance departments) and pre-approves all high school academic courses. When MA high schools submitted technology/engineering courses for review as science courses, NCAA rejected them because they were "vocational" rather than academic courses, no matter what evidence the school provided. And once a rejection letter was received, the guidance department had to tell the science and/or technology education department that the course could not be added to the school's program of studies for science credit. To address this issue, the Department wrote to NCAA explaining that the state has incorporated technology/engineering into science as an academic subject and asking that future requests be reviewed as such. NCAA agreed to do so and has now begun to approve these courses.

Implementation by Schools, Districts, and Institutions of Higher Education

Implementation Successes

Schools and districts have implemented a range of changes in the K–12 curriculum aligned with the technology/engineering standards. Although the Department has not collected unit lessons or syllabi, evidence of successful implementation can be seen in inquiries made by schools to the Department about implementation issues and curriculum development, newspaper articles about technology/engineering offerings, and students taking the high school technology/engineering MCAS test. The Department has also seen more district administrators taking an interest in technology/engineering, particularly those who follow state economic policy discussions where biotechnology and high-tech themes have been ongoing for several years now. Finally, the development of published curricula (primarily by the Museum) and textbooks aligned with state standards (e.g., by publishers Glencoe, Goodheart-Wilcox, and Great Lakes Press) have made it easier to initiate programs.

There have also been local successes in the recruitment of career changers to the teaching force. Districts are reporting success in hiring former engineers who have chosen to become teachers and engage in the development and teaching of technology/engineering programs. These teachers bring real-world experience to their instruction and a perspective that values the integration of traditional science topics and technology/engineering topics.

There have also been changes at the organizational level. A number of high schools have merged their science departments and technology education departments to create science and technology/engineering departments. The state's technology education professional organizations now explicitly include engineering in their mission statements and titles. The state's science fair organization also changed its name in 2006 to the Massachusetts State Science and Engineering Fair and increased the types of projects that can be submitted and judged.

Implementation Challenges

Schools and districts now can justify implementing technology/engineering programs through state policies. However, a number of implementation challenges must still be navigated. Distinguishing between technical and academic offerings is one challenge; local history and experience sometimes make transitioning technical programs to an academic focus difficult. As schools look around the state for examples and models, they are confronted by a wide range of programs and courses that vary in quality. They may also vary widely in design, because many of them were initially created by individuals. Until the science and technology education staff and organizations begin to collaborate in more specific ways, it is not clear whom teachers and schools should approach for support when they want to develop a program.

Once a program is established, another implementation issue confronting schools is the limited supply of certified teachers and the limited number of teacher preparation programs. Currently, there is only one teacher preparation program in the state, which graduates, on average, less than five new technology/engineering teachers per year. The Department is actively working to increase the number of preparation programs and offering support for initial technology/engineering licenses, but change like this will take time. Teacher preparation programs are hesitant to invest in program development until there is a demand for more teachers, but the demand has not been created, in part, because of the limited number of teachers available to design and implement K–12 programs.

Lessons Learned

The development of technology/engineering programs in Massachusetts provides a number of insights for others who may want to engage in similar efforts. The five lessons outlined below reflect the perspective of the author and are based on the particular circumstances in Massachusetts:

- Determine how the subject will be classified early on, because all policy decisions are based on that initial determination. For example, will engineering concepts be incorporated into a core academic subject, such as science, treated as an elective, or defined as a vocational discipline? Or will it be classified as a combination of these options?

- If engineering concepts are to be incorporated into core academic science, determine whether engineering will be a subject/strand of its own (as it is in Massachusetts) or a topic in other subjects/strands (some states have a "technological design" topic in each science subject). This decision will have significant policy implications for licensure and assessment.

- Determine the focus of the standards early on. Will they include only engineering concepts or technology education concepts (ITEA, 2000), or will they include a combination of the two?

- Provide examples of what the courses/curriculum will look like, and monitor development for quality and alignment. A number of resources are now available for schools to review.

- Focus on relationships. Mediate tensions between maintaining a "technology/engineering" identity and being folded into "science." Mediate tensions between "technologists" (technology educators) and "engineers." Encourage interaction between technology/engineering and science organizations early on so that everyone takes ownership of the new program.

Summary

The articulation of technology/engineering standards, the implementation of policies to support them, and programs to implement them have been an important undertaking for Massachusetts. Students now have the opportunity to participate in relevant, engaging, and what we consider necessary programs of study. We believe this will ultimately help meet our need for technologically literate citizens and a technical and engineering workforce. Groups and individuals throughout the educational system now support the implementation of technology/engineering standards, although change continues to be somewhat sporadic.

Massachusetts has worked diligently since 1993 to overcome a number of policy and implementation challenges. The first crucial step was the articulation of technology/engineering standards, as part of science. The efforts of professional organizations were crucial in making change happen, although closer attention to organizational relationships over the past 10 years would have helped to facilitate change. As the first state to include engineering concepts in state academic standards, we hope our experiences will be helpful to those making similar efforts in other states. The development of technology/engineering resources and programs is much more likely to be successful when many states are working toward a similar goal.

References

American Association for the Advancement of Science (AAAS). (1989). *Science for all Americans.* Washington, DC: Author.
American Association for the Advancement of Science (AAAS). (1993). *Benchmarks for science literacy.* New York: Oxford University Press.

International Technology Education Association (ITEA). (1996). *Technology for all Americans.* Reston, VA: Author.

International Technology Education Association (ITEA). (2000). *Standards for technological literacy: Content for the study of technology.* Reston, VA: Author.

Massachusetts Department of Elementary and Secondary Education (MA ESE). (1996). *Massachusetts Science and Technology Curriculum Framework.* Accessed at http://www.doe.mass.edu/frameworks/archive.html

Massachusetts Department of Elementary and Secondary Education (MA ESE). (2001). *Massachusetts Science and Technology/Engineering Curriculum Framework.* Accessed at http://www.doe.mass.edu/frameworks/current.html

Massachusetts General Laws, Chapter 69, Section 1D. Accessed at www.mass.gov/legis/laws/mgl/69-1d.htm

National Research Council (NRC). (1996). *National science education standards.* Washington, DC: National Academy Press.

U.S. Department of Education (USED), National Assessment Governing Board. (1996). *Science Framework for the 1996 National Assessment of Educational Progress.* Washington, DC: Author.

U.S. Department of Education (USED), National Assessment Governing Board. (2000). *Science Framework for the 1996 and 2000 National Assessment of Educational Progress.* Washington, DC: Author.

U.S. Department of Education (USED), National Assessment Governing Board. (2008). *Science Framework for the 2009 National Assessment of Educational Progress.* Washington, DC: Author.

**STANDARDS 2.0: NEW MODELS FOR THE NEW CENTURY:
ALTERNATIVES TO TRADITIONAL CONTENT STANDARDS**

James Rutherford

"Only when we agree about what all high school graduates need to be successful
will we be able to tackle the most significant challenge ahead of us:
transforming instruction for every child,"[4]

"Common standards are a crucial first step toward putting our country's children
on the road to international competitiveness."[5]

The statements above were made in the context of an effort—involving 46 states and the District
of Columbia—just launched by the National Governors Association (NGA) and the Council of
Chief State School Officers (CCSSO)[6] to create a common core of voluntary state standards in
English language and mathematics. These efforts can be taken as evidence that the standards
movement is not going away anytime soon, never mind the lack of solid evidence that content
standards have an important impact on K–12 education. For most educators, the notion that we
should understand as clearly as possible what we want all students to learn still makes sense.

Note that this new standards undertaking focuses on English and math, which is not surprising
because those subjects will always be at the top of the school reform hierarchy. It follows that it
will be some time before states get around to forging common standards for second-tier subjects
(science, history, etc.), let alone engineering. Thus engineering need not rush to come up with
national K–12 engineering education standards. Instead it can afford to take deliberate steps to
find its desired place in the school curriculum, steps that will result in the evolution of
engineering standards rather than their instantaneous birth.

Notice also that the NGA/CCSSO project does nothing to change the structure of the curriculum
structure. Since the end of the World War II, the K–12 curriculum has steadily added content but
removed very little. The curriculum is now so over-stuffed that there is little or no room for the
likes of engineering, environment, or economics content. Nonetheless, teachers and publishers
are reluctant to deal with content overload by simple surgery,[7] so year to year content learning
demands expand, the curricular structure remains rigidly fixed, and coherence declines.[8]
Sometime in this century the curriculum will have to be dramatically redesigned *structurally* to

---

[4] CCSSO President-Elect and Maine Education Commissioner Sue Gendron. www.ccsso.org.
[5] Editorial, *San Francisco Chronicle*, June 8, 2009.
[6] Partnering with The College Board and ACT.
[7] The AAAS Project 2061's *Designs for Science Literacy* has a chapter, "Unburdening the Curriculum,"
that identifies major topics and technical language that can be cut from the science courses, subtopics that
can be trimmed from remaining major topics. As far as I know, none of the textbook publishers or
classroom teachers has followed this advice.
[8] Check out today's textbooks. In the sciences they are monsters approaching 1000 pages, and don't even
tell an engaging story.

enable a coherent, conceptually rich, standards-based curriculum to emerge. Engineering is positioned to lead in the design of this radical 21st century reform.[9]

So Here We Go

My idea is that the engineering community not only work toward increasing its presence in the schools, but that it do so in a way that provides the nation with the capacity to create curricula that respond to 21st-century needs in a 21st-century way.

Step 1. Establish an independent education center dedicated to providing the ideas and leadership necessary to design and oversee the installation of a 21st-century curricular *structure* and to foster the meaningful presence of engineering in school curricula. The board, affiliates, and panels of this education center would include representatives of industrial and academic engineering, education policy makers, administrators, and teachers, and university facility.[10] The following steps will proceed pretty much in parallel.

Step 2. Conceptualize a design (including specifications) for a new publication, *Engineering for All Americans.* The purpose of this publication would be to tell the engineering education story in a captivating way for educators and citizens and to provide a conceptual base for other resources to follow. *Science for All Americans* might well serve as a model.[11] The design concept would be used to seek funding, and if successful, the project would proceed.

Step 3. Create design specifications (i.e., standards) for Engineering Context Teaching Modules. The purpose of these modules would be to help teachers teach their *current* subjects, not engineering. Develop a few samples. Encourage teachers and engineers to create additional examples following the given design standards. *Resources for Science Literacy*, developed by the Environmental Literacy Council and the National Science Teachers Association, can serve as a model.[12] The creation of standards would increase the presence of engineering in the schools in a positive way and, therefore, would not be seen as an effort to displace current subjects.

Step 4. Establish a capacity for systematically reviewing engineering education instructional materials (print and Internet) for accuracy and for relevance to K–12 education. As an organization, the Environmental Literacy Council, which started out reviewing instructional materials, found that authors and publishers often responded by making changes in the content. The process of reaching agreement on review criteria would necessarily lead to decisions related to standards.

Step 5. Create standards for "curriculum blocks." Middle school and high school courses and elementary school subjects were the building blocks of 20th century school curricula. At some point in this century, the building blocks will become much more varied, will reflect much

---

[9] Design, after all, is the business of engineering.
[10] I realize that this could be politically difficult, but in the absence of the equivalent of an AAAS, a consortium of some sort will be needed.
[11] www.project2061.org
[12] www.envirolit.org

more integration of disciplines, and will be assembled in a variety of ways using CAD/CAM to yield desired learning outcomes. (See About Curriculum Blocks below)

Step 6. Design and set in operation a computer facility for designing K–12 curricula and managing resources. [13] A computer facility, accessible on the Internet, would allow curriculum developers to search the "warehouse" of curriculum blocks in various ways, to assemble a set that meets their goals and constraints, to manage associated materials, and continuously collect feedback from teachers to share with the block developers. This is technologically feasible, but strong technical, managerial, and political leadership will be needed to create the facility and to phase it in over the next 25 or so years.[14]

As all of these steps progress, an analysis of the emerging standards (implicit as well as explicit) of the engineering education materials being developed should provide an experiential basis for developing overarching Engineering Education Standards.

About Curriculum Blocks[15]

A curriculum block is a self-contained sequence of instruction that could be taught in a range of time dimensions and instructional formats, could relate to one discipline or several, and would be fully described to enable curriculum designers to make informed choices. Among the possibilities are: design blocks; case-study blocks; design-challenge blocks; domain cross-cutting blocks; explanation blocks; inquiry blocks; issue blocks; theme-concept blocks; and so on. To ensure that these blocks are not formulated willy-nilly, design standards will be necessary to guide their construction. Descriptions of curriculum blocks should include the following information:

- **Overview.** Which students the block is designed for; school subject area; how instruction is organized; time frame; required prior knowledge and skills; rationale.
- **Content.** Specific learning goals; main topics; activities; links to subsequent or parallel parts of the curriculum.
- **Operation.** Human resource requirements; material resource requirements; how assessment will be carried out; cost in time and money.
- **Credibility.** Empirical evaluation of learning outcomes; published reviews by independent experts; information about where the block is being used; when and by whom the block was developed.

What This Adds Up To

My suggestions amount to linking two propositions. The engineering community should (1) create standards for engineering-related instructional materials; and (2) take the lead in designing the structure of the 21st-century K–12 curriculum. These two components must go hand in hand.

---

[13] See *Designs for Science Literacy*, Prologue, and Chapters 1, 2, & 3

[14] This is not long. Recall that the Sputnik-era reforms took place nearly 50 years ago, *A Nation at Risk* 26 years ago, and Project 2061 will have its 25th birthday next year.

[15] See *Designs for Science Literacy*, pp. 123–47.

I believe the engineering community can increase the presence of engineering education in the schools more effectively by setting standards for, and providing for the development of, a new generation of instructional materials by developing national engineering education standards at this time. These materials can be engineering modules that help teachers teach their subjects more interestingly, engineering case studies that bring together information and concepts from several disciplines, and engineering units that organize content around cross-cutting themes, such as scale or systems analysis. A concerted, ongoing effort involving hundreds of engineers and teachers over many years can eventually lead to consensus on learning standards.

Computers are powerful design tools, and it is time they were used to assist in reshaping the K–12 curriculum for modern times. Engineers are experts in using computers to design complex systems, such as the Boeing 777 and international communication networks, so why not use them for the K–12 curriculum? In our world today, the challenge of education increases relentlessly, but at the same time computers and the Internet are changing where, when, how, and what kind of learning can take place. The curriculum must be reshaped accordingly.

The engineering community can take the lead in making that a reality.

Towards a Vision for Integrating Engineering
into Science and Mathematics Standards

Cary Sneider, Portland State University
Linda P. Rosen, Education and Management Innovations, Inc.

June 26, 2009

Abstract

Improved education standards will not, by themselves, lead to the scientifically and technologically literate citizenry we need for our nation to prosper in the 21st century. However, as we've learned in virtually every other professional field, standards can be an important first step toward changes that will lead to excellence and equity. It is now widely accepted that all students need a fundamental conceptual understanding and abilities in science, technology, engineering, and mathematics (STEM), but of those four, only science and mathematics have been given reserved places in the K–12 curriculum. Unfortunately, previous efforts to integrate technology and engineering into science and mathematics standards have met with limited success. Most science educators have focused only on aspects of national standards directly related to science disciplines. And mathematics educators' interests in technology have been limited to tools for computation. Given that history, it is an open question whether or not a new generation of science and mathematics standards that include technology and engineering would bring about a different result. Although we cannot answer that question at present, we can consider how to go about developing a new vision of technology and engineering standards consistent with the "fewer, higher, clearer" guidelines that are driving the development of the next generation of standards. In the process we touch on three themes: definitions of technology and engineering, the content of current technology and engineering frameworks, and a strategy for integrating these standards into core academic subjects so they will be viewed as essential complements, rather than optional add-ons, to those disciplines.

Introduction

Although a movement in support of national standards has been under way for 20 years (since the publication of *Curriculum and Evaluation Standards for School Mathematics* 1989 and *Science for All Americans* [SFAA] in 1990), our American penchant for states' rights has led each state to develop its own unique standards. The results have been roundly criticized as too broad, vague, repetitive, and poorly coordinated to define coherent guidance for textbook developers, assessment specialists, and teachers to follow (Beatty, 2008). Moreover, the sheer number of different types of standards intended to guide the work of generalist teachers (especially many K-5 teachers) has made mastery unlikely (Hudson et al., 2002, and Appendix A, p. 135).

Growing concern over the dismal performance of our students on national and international tests in mathematics and science and recognition that a patchwork of educational standards is at least partly to blame has led to a call for common state standards. Although still resistant to "federal" standards, state-elected officials are warming to the idea of "common standards" that would address the worst problems of the current system while allowing states to retain some control over content in their own jurisdictions. At the time of this writing, 46 states have agreed in principle to adopt common standards in English and mathematics (McNeil, 2009), and science is likely to be next on the agenda.

The prospect of a next generation of educational standards means there may be an opportunity to integrate technology and engineering standards. However, there is still no universal agreement on the meaning of "technology" and "engineering," let alone on a vision for how these subjects can, or should, be integrated into our K–12 system. Given the current call for fewer, clearer, higher standards and the difficulty of adding entirely new courses of study, especially at the high school level, it is unlikely that a separate set of standards for technology or engineering would be widely adopted by the states. Consequently, our best bet is to develop a clear, coherent vision of exemplary standards in technology and engineering and then consider how they might fit into traditional K–12 subjects.

Developing a vision for fewer, clearer, higher engineering standards could be undertaken in a number of ways. One approach would be to convene a workshop of engineers, educators, and experts in related fields to determine the most important concepts and abilities that everyone needs to be an effective citizen, worker, and/or consumer. That was the approach in chapters 3 and 8 of SFAA in the 1980s, and it is the approach being taken now by the team writing a framework for technological literacy for the National Assessment of Educational Progress.

A second approach would be to comb the international literature, using sources such as *Technology's Challenge to Science Education* (Layton, 1993), which chronicles the evolution of technology in the national curriculum of England and Wales, and the series *Innovations in Science and Technology Education* (UNESCO, Volumes I–VIII, 1986–2003), which describe similar efforts in many industrialized and developing nations. One purpose of this search would be to determine whether or not there is an existence proof for national standards that fully integrate technology and engineering into core subjects, and if so, what its characteristics are.

A third approach is to start with the standards that already exist in the United States and imagine how they might be shaped in their next iteration so that they are perceived by practitioners as essential to core subjects. Ideally, all three methods could be "triangulated" to produce a set of optimal engineering standards.

Given limited time, this paper will skim the surface of the third approach by providing an overview of engineering standards in current frameworks and suggesting a potential approach to synthesizing earlier efforts. We turn first to definitions of terms used in educational contexts.

Definitions of Technology and Engineering Education

SFAA (AAAS, 1990) was the first major document to provide a broad vision for science education that included a major role for technology and engineering. These terms were defined as follows:

> In the broadest sense, technology extends our abilities to change the world: to cut, shape, or put together materials; to move things from one place to another; to reach farther with our hands, voices, and senses. We use technology to try to change the world to suit us better. The changes may relate to survival needs such as food, shelter, or defense, or they may relate to human aspirations such as knowledge, art, or control. But the results of changing the world are often complicated and unpredictable. They can include unexpected benefits, unexpected costs, and unexpected risks—any of which may fall on different social groups at different times. Anticipating the effects of technology is therefore as important as advancing its capabilities. . . .

> Engineering, the systematic application of scientific knowledge in developing and applying technology, has grown from a craft to become a science in itself. Scientific knowledge provides a

means of estimating what the behavior of things will be even before we make them or observe them. Moreover, science often suggests new kinds of behavior that had not even been imagined before, and so leads to new technologies. Engineers use knowledge of science and technology, together with strategies of design, to solve practical problems. (AAAS, 1990, p. 23–24)

The definition of technology and its proposed role in the schools was further developed in *Benchmarks for Science Literacy* (AAAS, 1993):

Technology is an overworked term. It once meant knowing how to do things—the practical arts or the study of the practical arts. But it has also come to mean innovations such as pencils, television, aspirin, microscopes, etc., that people use for specific purposes, and it refers to human activities such as agriculture or manufacturing and even to processes such as animal breeding or voting or war that change certain aspects of the world. Further, technology sometimes refers to the industrial and military institutions dedicated to producing and using inventions and know-how. (AAAS, 1993, p. 43)

In *The National Science Education Standards* ([NSES]; NRC, 1996), technology was given a prominent place in science education, and a distinction was made between scientific inquiry and technological design:

Although these are science education standards, the relationship between science and technology is so close that any presentation of science without developing an understanding of technology would portray an inaccurate picture of science. (NRC, 1996, p. 190)

As used in the Standards, the central distinguishing characteristic between science and technology is a difference in goal: The goal of science is to understand the natural world, and the goal of technology is to make modifications in the world to meet human needs. Technology as design is included in the Standards as parallel to science as inquiry. (NRC, 1996, p. 24)

NSES also differentiated the roles of scientists and engineers:

Scientists propose explanations for questions about the natural world, and *engineers* propose solutions relating to human problems, needs, and aspirations. (NSES, p. 166)

In contrast to the science documents, which define technology broadly, mathematics documents define technology much more narrowly as electronic tools:

Calculators and other technological tools, such as computer algebra systems, interactive geometry software, applets, spreadsheets, and interactive presentation devices, are vital components of a high-quality mathematics education. With guidance from effective mathematics teachers, students at different levels can use these tools to support and extend mathematical reasoning and sense making, gain access to mathematical content and problem-solving contexts, and enhance computational fluency. In a well-articulated mathematics program, students can use these tools for computation, construction, and representation as they explore problems. The use of technology also contributes to mathematical reflection, problem identification, and decision making. (NCTM, 2008)

In brief, mathematics documents use the term "technology" to refer to modern electronic tools. They do not typically refer to engineering at all, except as one of many fields that require mathematics. The science frameworks use the term "technology" to refer to all of the ways natural materials are modified to meet human needs and desires. Mathematics documents distinguish between science and technology, and scientists and engineers, primarily by differences in their goals. This distinction is concisely stated in the following quote attributed to the famous engineer Theodore von Karman: The scientist seeks to understand what is, the engineer seeks to create what never was (Petroski, 1997).

Additional insights about the relationship between science and technology in education and the distinct role of engineering emerges from a series of papers delivered at UNESCO conferences in the 1970s on the question of how to organize science and technology education in developing countries. For example, Harold Foecke, then director of pre-university science and technology education for UNESCO, urged attendees to teach science and technology together as basic education for all students. He made the distinction between science and technology (and between scientist and engineer) as one of motivating forces [goals], processes, and products:

Motivating forces [goals]: In science to know, explain, and predict, and in technology to find new and better ways of doing things;

Processes: In science the research process proceeds from the particular to the general, and in technology the design, problem-solving or decision-making process proceeds from the general to the particular; and

Products: Science results in new knowledge about the natural and man-made worlds while technology produces new materials, devices, techniques, processes, and systems to serve human needs.

Another of Foecke's themes concerns the role of engineers in society. In one paper, he lists many of the problems that plague humankind—natural disasters, shortages of food and water, disease, air and water pollution, and so on.

With respect to these human problems the scientists' role is to find out what is. The technologist's role is to determine what can be, and the engineer's role is to recommend what should be. Because the engineer's role in decision-making may profoundly affect society, engineers need to be well educated in the humanities and social sciences as well as in science, mathematics, and engineering design" (Foecke, 1970).

A third theme that emerges from this literature is a strategy for including science and technology as distinct but related subjects for all citizens. In *Fifty Years of UNESCO Leadership in Science and Technology Education*, Foecke (1995) explains that the introduction of technology as part of general education grew out of earlier efforts by UNESCO to integrate various fields of science into courses of study that have practical value at all pre-university levels. However, initial efforts to introduce technology as separate courses in the curriculum were resisted because they were incorrectly perceived as "vocational," and some educators thought they were inappropriate for college-bound students. Consequently, UNESCO adopted a strategy of integrating technology education and science education, while preserving the distinctions between science and technology. We will return to the question of strategy later. First, we will look at technology and engineering in current national and state standards documents.

Table 1. *Benchmarks for Science Literacy*: **Chapter 3B Design and Systems**

Grades K–2	People can use objects and ways of doing things to solve problems. People may not be able to actually make or do everything they design.
Grades 3–5	There is no perfect design. Designs that are best in one respect (safety or ease of use, for example) may be inferior in other ways (cost or appearance). Usually some features must be sacrificed to get others. How such trade-offs are received depends on which features are emphasized and which are down-played. Even a good design may fail. Sometimes steps can be taken ahead of time to reduce the likelihood of failure, but it cannot be truly eliminated. The solution to one problem may create other problems.
Grades 6–8	Design usually requires taking constraints into account. Some constraints, such as gravity or the properties of the materials to be used, are unavoidable. Other constraints, including economic, political, social, ethical, and aesthetic ones, limit choices. All technologies have effects other than those intended by the design, some of which may have been predictable and some not. In either case, these side effects may turn out to be unacceptable to some of the population and therefore lead to conflict between groups. Almost all control systems have inputs, outputs, and feedback. The essence of control is comparing information about what is happening to what people want to happen and then making appropriate adjustments. This procedure requires sensing information, processing it, and making changes. In almost all modern machines, microprocessors serve as centers of performance control. Systems fail because they have faulty or poorly matched parts, are used in ways that exceed what was intended by the design, or were poorly designed to begin with. The most common ways to prevent failure are pretesting parts and procedures, overdesign, and redundancy.
Grades 9–12	In designing a device or process, thought should be given to how it will be manufactured, operated, maintained, replaced, and disposed of and who will sell, operate, and take care of it. The costs associated with these functions may introduce yet more constraints on the design. The value of any given technology may be different for different groups of people and at different points in time. Complex systems have layers of controls. Some controls operate particular parts of the system and some control other controls. Even fully automatic systems require human control at some point. Risk analysis is used to minimize the likelihood of unwanted side effects of a new technology. The public perception of risk may depend, however, on psychological factors as well as scientific ones. The more parts and connections a system has, the more ways it can go wrong. Complex systems usually have components to detect, back up, bypass, or compensate for minor failures. To reduce the chance of system failure, performance testing is often conducted using small-scale models, computer simulations, analogous systems, or just the parts of the system thought to be least reliable.

Technology and Engineering in National Science Standards

Benchmarks for Science Literacy (AAAS, 1993), the first set of science education standards in the United States, describes what students should know in grades K–2, 3–5, 6–8, and 9–12. Chapter 3, The Nature of Technology, consists of three parts: Technology and Society; Design and Systems; and Issues in Technology. Chapter 8, The Designed World, consists of six parts: Agriculture, Materials and Manufacturing, Energy Sources and Use, Communication, Information Processing, and Health Technology. Although all of this material is relevant to understanding engineering and technology, in the interests of brevity, Table 1 presents just the benchmarks in Chapter 3B, Design and Systems, which are closest to the heart of engineering. Notice that benchmark is described in a declarative statement. Although the authors of *Benchmarks* indicate that they expect students to learn by engaging in design and technology projects, their focus is on what students should *know* about engineering.

The *National Science Education Standards (NSES)* (NRC, 1996) was developed in response to a perceived need for a clear set of goals. At the time, only a few states had educational standards, and *Benchmarks* was one of just two national documents in circulation in the early 1990s. The National Science Teachers Association initiated the *Scope, Sequence and Coordination* (SS&C) Project to replace the "layer cake" approach of teaching biology, chemistry, and physics in separate courses. The SS&C approach was to replace the entire middle school and high school curriculum with a coordinated sequence of science units so that students would be taking all of the sciences every year. Concepts in each scientific field would build from year to year, and within a given year students would have opportunities to understand how different fields of science were related to each other. These concepts were laid out in a set of standards called the *Content Core*. Many science educators chose to follow the SS&C route, while others followed the *Benchmarks* approach. Confusion between the two approaches led to a request to the National Research Council to bring the leaders of the science education community and scientists together to develop a definitive set of standards for the nation.

NSES, developed with input and support from the creators of the AAAS documents, and many others, also gave technology and engineering a prominent place in science. However, the scope was considerably diminished in comparison with SFAA and *Benchmarks*. Perhaps because SFAA and *Benchmarks* had been criticized for being too broad, NSES limited the inclusion of technology and engineering to concepts and abilities explicitly linked to science:

> The science and technology standards in Table 6.5 establish connections between the natural and design worlds and provide students with opportunities to develop decision-making abilities. They are not standards for technology education; rather these standards emphasize abilities associated with the process of design and fundamental understandings about the enterprise of science and its various linkages with technology.

Nonetheless, many statements in NSES about what students should know and be able to do are similar to those in *Benchmarks*. Also, statements about technology are divided into two sections: (1) what students should know about technology and (2) what they should be able to do. The latter are summarized in Table 2.

Table 2. *National Science Education Standards*: **Abilities of Technological Design**

Grades K–4	**Identify a simple problem:** In problem identification, children should develop the ability to explain a problem in their own words and identify a specific task and solution related to the problem.
	Propose a solution. Students should make proposals to build something or get something to work better; they should be able to describe and communicate their ideas. Students should recognize that designing a solution might have constraints, such as cost, materials, time, space, or safety.
	Implementing proposed solutions. Children should develop abilities to work individually and collaboratively and to use suitable tools, techniques, and quantitative measurements when appropriate. Students should demonstrate the ability to balance simple constraints in problem solving.
	Evaluate a product or design. Students should evaluate their own results or solutions to problems, as well as those of other children, by considering how well a product or design met the challenge to solve a problem. When possible, students should use measurements and include constraints and other criteria in their evaluations. They should modify designs based on the results of evaluations.
	Communicate a problem, design, and solution. Student abilities should include oral, written, and pictorial communication of the design process and product. The communication might be show and tell, group discussions, short written reports, or pictures, depending on the students' abilities and the design project.
Grades 5–8	**Identify appropriate problems for technological design.** Students should develop their abilities by identifying a specified need, considering its various aspects, and talking to different potential users or beneficiaries. They should appreciate that for some needs, the cultural backgrounds and beliefs of different groups can affect the criteria for a suitable product.
	Design a solution or product. Students should make and compare different proposals in the light of the criteria they have selected. They must consider constraints—such as cost, time, trade-offs, and materials needed—and communicate ideas with drawings and simple models.
	Implement a proposed design. Students should organize materials and other resources, plan their work, make good use of group collaboration where appropriate, choose suitable tools and techniques, and work with appropriate measurement methods to ensure adequate accuracy.
	Evaluate completed technological designs or products. Students should use criteria relevant to the original purpose of need, consider a variety of factors that might affect acceptability and suitability for intended users or beneficiaries, and develop measures of quality with respect to such criteria and factors; they should also suggest improvements for their own products, try proposed modifications.
	Communicate the process of technological design. Students should review and describe any completed piece of work and identify the stages of problem identification, solution design, implementation, and evaluation.
Grades 9–12	**Identify a problem or design an opportunity.** Students should be able to identify new problems or needs and to change and improve current technological designs.
	Propose designs and choose between alternative solutions. Students should demonstrate thoughtful planning for a piece of technology or technique. Students should be introduced to the roles of models and simulations in these processes.
	Implement a proposed solution. A variety of skills can be needed in proposing a solution depending on the type of technology that is involved. The construction of artifacts can require the skills of cutting, shaping, treating, and joining common materials—such as wood, metal, plastics, and textiles. Solutions can also be implemented using computer software.
	Evaluate the solution and its consequences. Students should test any solution against the needs and criteria it was designed to meet. At this stage, new criteria not originally considered may be reviewed.
	Communicate the problem, process, and solution. Students should present their results to students, teachers, and others in a variety of ways, such as orally, in writing, and in other forms—including models, diagrams, and demonstrations.

Standards for Technological Literacy (STL) (ITEA, 2000) proposes perhaps the most fully developed standards for technology and engineering education. The document was developed by the International Technology Education Association in collaboration with the National Academy of Engineering. STL is an organized set of 20 standards patterned largely on the framework of SFAA and *Benchmarks*, but elaborated more fully. The 20 standards are broken down into benchmarks for grades K–2, 3–5, 6–8, and 9–12 and grouped into five major areas, as shown below:

The Nature of Technology
   1. The characteristics and scope of technology.
   2. The core concepts of technology.
   3. The relationships among technologies and connections with other fields.
Technology and Society
   4. The cultural, social, economic and political effects of technology.
   5. The effects of technology on the environment.
   6. The role of society in the development and use of technology.
   7. The influence of technology on history.
Design
   8. The attributes of design.
   9. Engineering design.
   10. The role of troubleshooting, R&D, invention, innovation and experimentation in problem solving.
Abilities for a Technological World
   11. Apply the design process.
   12. Use and maintain technological products and systems.
   13. Assess the impact of products and systems.
The Designed World
   14. Medical technologies.
   15. Agricultural and related biotechnologies.
   16. Energy and power technologies.
   17. Information and communication technologies.
   18. Transportation technologies.
   19. Manufacturing technologies.
   20. Construction technologies.

Notice that standards 1–13 correspond to many of the ideas in *Benchmarks* Chapter 3, The Nature of Technology, and that standards 14-20 correspond to *Benchmarks* Chapter 8, The Designed World. However, the detailed descriptions of what students are expected to know and be able to do are more explicit in STL than in *Benchmarks*.

Although STL is now almost a decade old, it remains the most comprehensive set of standards for technology and engineering education yet developed and should provide an excellent pool from which to draw ideas for the next generation of standards. The standards that primarily concern engineering are 8, 9, 10 (all under "Design"), and 11 (classified under "Abilities for a Technological World"). These are shown in Table 3.

Table 3 *Standards for Technological Literacy*: **Standards 8, 9, 10, and 11**

	Standard 8. Students will develop an understanding of the attributes of design.
Grades K–2	Everyone can design solutions to a problem. Design is a creative process.
Grades 3–5	The design process is a purposeful method of planning practical solutions to problems. Requirements for a design include such factors as the desired elements and features of a product or system or the limits that are placed on the design.
Grades 6–8	Design is a creative planning process that leads to useful products and systems. There is no perfect design. Requirements for design are made up of criteria and constraints.
Grades 9–12	The design process includes defining a problem, brainstorming, researching and generating ideas, identifying criteria and specifying constraints, exploring possibilities, selecting an approach, developing a design proposal, making a model or prototype, testing and evaluating the design using specifications, refining the design, creating or making it, and communicating processes and results. Design problems are seldom presented in a clearly defined form. The design needs to be continually checked and critiqued, and the ideas of the design must be redefined and improved. Requirements of a design, such as criteria, constraints, and efficiency, sometime compete with each other.
	Standard 9. Students will develop an understanding of engineering design.
Grades K–2	The engineering design process includes identifying a problem, looking for ideas, developing solutions, and sharing solutions with others. Expressing ideas to others verbally and through sketches and models is an important part of the design process.
Grades 3–5	The engineering design process involves defining a problem, generating ideas, selecting a solution, testing the solution(s), making the item, evaluating it, and presenting the results. When designing an object, it is important to be creative and consider all ideas. Models are used to communicate and test design ideas and processes.
Grades 6–8	Design involves a set of steps, which can be performed in different sequences and repeated as needed. Brainstorming is a group problem-solving design process in which each person in the group presents his or her ideas in an open forum. Modeling, testing, evaluating, and modifying are used to transform ideas into practical solutions.
Grades 9–12	Established design principles are used to evaluate existing designs, to collect data, and to guide the design process. Engineering design is influenced by personal characteristics, such as creativity, resourcefulness, and the ability to visualize and think abstractly. A prototype is a working model used to test a design concept by making actual observations and necessary adjustments. The process of engineering design takes into account a number of factors.

	Standard 10. Students will develop an understanding of the role of troubleshooting, research and development, invention and innovation, and experimentation in problem solving.
Grades K–2	Asking questions and making observations helps a person to figure out how things work.
	All products and systems are subject to failure. Many products and systems, however, can be fixed.
Grades 3–5	Troubleshooting is a way of finding out why something does not work so that it can be fixed.
	Invention and innovation are creative ways to turn ideas into real things.
	The process of experimentation, which is common in science, can help solve technological problems.
Grades 6–8	Troubleshooting is a problem-solving method used to identify the cause of a malfunction in a technological system.
	Invention is a process of turning ideas and imagination into devices and systems.
	Innovation is the process of modifying an existing product or system to improve it.
	Some technological problems are best solved through experimentation.
Grades 9–12	Research and development is a specific problem-solving approach that is used intensively in business and industry to prepare devices and systems for the marketplace.
	Technological problems must be researched before they can be solved.
	Not all problems are technological, and not every problem can be solved using technology.
	Many technological problems require a multidisciplinary approach.
	Standard 11. Students will develop the abilities to apply the design process.
Grades K–2	Brainstorm people's needs and wants and pick problems that can be solved through the design process.
	Build or construct an object using the design process.
	Investigate how things are made and how they can be improved.
Grades 3–5	Identify and collect information about everyday problems that can be solved by technology, and generate ideas and requirements for solving a problem.
	The process of designing involves presenting some possible solutions in visual form and then selecting the best solution(s) from many.
	Test and evaluate the solutions for the design problem.
	Improve the design solutions.
Grades 6–8	Apply a design process to solve problems in and beyond the laboratory-classroom.
	Specify criteria and constraints for the design.
	Make two-dimensional and three-dimensional representations of the designed solution.
	Test and evaluate the design in relation to pre-established requirements, such as criteria and constraints, and refine as needed.
	Make a product or system and document the solution.
Grades 9–12	Identify the design problem to solve and decide whether or not to address it.
	Identify criteria and constraints and determine how these will affect the design process.
	Refine a design by using prototypes and modeling to ensure quality, efficiency, and productivity.
	Evaluate the design solution using conceptual, physical, and mathematical models at various intervals of the design process to check for proper design and to note areas where improvements are needed.
	Develop and produce a product or system using a design process.
	Evaluate final solutions and communicate observation, processes, and results of the design process, using verbal, graphic, quantitative, virtual, and written means, in addition to three-dimensional models.

Engineering Frameworks for a High School Setting (Koehler et al., 2005), updated engineering standards, is an attempt to improve on the engineering standards in *Benchmarks*, NSES, and STL. The document is similar in many ways to previous frameworks that focused only on high school engineering standards. This document uses the following outline:

I. Content Standards

    A. Information and Communication

        1. Instruments

        2. Mediums

    B. Sources of Power/Energy

    C. Transportation

    D. Food and Medicine

        1. Engineering in Food

        2. Engineering in Medicine

II. Engineering Tools

    A. Engineering Paradigm [engineering design process]

    B. Science and Mathematics

    C. Social Studies

    D. Computer Tools

Part I is similar to the content in Chapter 8 ,The Designed World, from *Benchmarks*, whereas Part II is similar to Chapter 3, The Nature of Technology, and "Technology and Science" in NSES. Because Part II seemed to be closest in spirit to the engineering standards described previously, these have been included in Table 4. The authors of this framework used it successfully to compare the content of standards in 49 states (Koehler et al., 2006).

Table 4. *Engineering Frameworks for a High School Setting*: **Part II Tools**

A. The Engineering Paradigm is a systematic methodology that allows a technically literate person to gain perspective into the logical decomposition of a problem and its iterative procedure toward a solution. The topics covered in these content standards can only be explicitly understood in this context. More specifically, this is the fundamental tool for exploration, understanding, and improvement of the content covered in the Standards. In addition, this Engineering Paradigm provides an analytical thought process that can be extended to addressing other problems beyond the traditional scope of engineering and technology. Finally, it is imperative that a technically literate society be able to compare and contrast the products that it uses. This paradigm enables consumers to evaluate the functionality and capabilities of products in terms of design optimization and the trade-offs inherent in satisfying multiple constraints. This paradigm is outlined below. • Problem recognition and definition • Problem decomposition • Piecewise analysis • Preemptive generation of possible solutions • Consideration of constraints • Iterative revision of possible solutions • Iterative prototyping until an acceptable product • Final design optimization
B. Science and Mathematics. All technology is ultimately derived from the application of scientific and mathematical principles. Therefore, a solid foundation in these disciplines is essential for facilitating a comprehensive understanding of the content standards. The following should be covered in the course of a high school education. • Science Disciplines Math Topics • Biology Geometry • Chemistry Algebra • Physics Trigonometry • Calculus
C. Social Sciences. Engineering, as a discipline, is focused on improving society by satisfying its ever-changing technological needs. Thus, while technology is derived from scientific and mathematical principles, its development is predominantly driven by sociological motivation and constraints. It is important that these factors be considered in the study of any technical system. Furthermore, the Engineering Paradigm outlines an iterative approach toward final design optimization. This process is by no means limited to technical constraints but must also satisfy its sociological requirements. It is important that the Content Standards, and their sociological optimization, are studied in the context of sociology, economics, ethics, and politics
D. Computer Tools. Our society is inextricably bound to the computer infrastructure that supports it. Technical literacy thus increasingly requires proficiency with various computer tools and applications to effectively interact within our technologically advanced environment. However, the engineering community is absolutely dependent on its computer tools for system development. Because of the complexity of these systems, such as those covered in the Content Standards, the use of computer tools greatly enhances their meaningful and thorough exploration. Students should have a working knowledge of the following computer tools. General computing Word processing Spreadsheet Communication tools Presentation tools Familiarity with operating systems Computer programming Algorithmic synthesis and decomposition Implementation of computer-based models Computer aided drafting / drawing

Technology and Engineering in National Mathematics Standards

An Agenda for Action (NCTM 1980), released in response to the "back to basics" movement of the late 1970s, became the first major document to set out a vision of mathematics education for modern times. The *Agenda* called for an emphasis on problem solving over drill and practice and encouraged mathematics educators to use calculators and computers with students in the earliest practical grade. Other recommendations included the creation of student-centered classrooms where students could explore mathematical concepts rather than complete worksheets. The message on computational technology was clear: the K–12 mathematics curriculum should take advantage of calculating devices rather than sticking with the traditional paper-and-pencil algorithms. In this report, the mathematics education community first equated knowledge of technology with knowledge of appropriate use of calculators and computers.

Curriculum and Evaluation Standards for School Mathematics (NCTM 1989) was developed by a mathematics education community that had become weary of the pendulum swings in mathematics curriculum between basics and reform and the focus on the best and brightest. The purpose of this document was to proactively define what all students should know and be able to do. The National Council of Teachers of Mathematics (NCTM) Commission overseeing the task had two charges:

> Create a coherent vision of what it means to be mathematically literate both in a world that relies on calculators and computers to carry out mathematical procedures and in a world where mathematics is rapidly growing and is extensively applied in diverse fields.

> Create a set of standards to guide the revision of the school mathematics curriculum and its associated evaluation toward this vision. (NCTM, 1989, p. 1)

The document that emerged was more detailed about how teachers should teach than it was on the specific content students should learn. Three aspects of mathematics are featured in the document:

- . . . "knowing" mathematics is "doing" mathematics. A person gathers, discovers, or creates knowledge in the course of some activity having a purpose. . . .

- The Computer's ability to process large sets of information has made quantification and the logical analysis of information possible in such areas as business, economics, linguistics, biology, medicine, and sociology...However, the fundamental mathematical ideas needed in these areas are not necessarily those studied in the traditional algebra-geometry-precalculus-calculus sequence, a sequence designed with engineering and physical science applications in mind. Because mathematics is a foundation discipline for other disciplines and grows in direct proportion to its utility, we believe that the curriculum for all students must provide opportunities to develop an understanding of mathematical models, structures, and simulations applicable to many disciplines.

- Changes in technology and the broadening of the areas in which mathematics is applied have resulted in growth and changes in the discipline of mathematics itself...The new technology not only has made calculations and graphing easier, it has changed the very nature of the problems important to mathematics and the methods mathematicians use to investigate them. (NCTM, 1989, pp. 7–8)

In one of the few overt references to engineering (cited above), the *Curriculum and Evaluation Standards* deliberately seeks to expand the mathematical pre-college curriculum beyond the educational needs of prospective scientists and engineers. Nonetheless, the following standards have some relevance to engineering education, even though they are not described from such a perspective.

Table 5: *Curriculum Standards in School Mathematics*

	Mathematics as problem-solving
Grades K–4	The study of mathematics should emphasize problem solving so that students can: • Use problem-solving approaches to investigate and understand mathematical content; • Formulate problems from everyday and mathematical situations; • Develop and apply strategies to solve a wide variety of problems; • Verify and interpret results with respect to the original problem; • Acquire confidence in using mathematics meaningfully.
Grades 5–8	The mathematics curriculum should include numerous and varied experiences with problem solving as a method of inquiry and application so that students can: • Use problem-solving approaches to investigate and understand mathematical content; • Formulate problems from situations within and outside mathematics; • Develop and apply a variety of strategies to solve problems, with emphasis on multistep and non-routine problems. • Verify and interpret results with respect to the original problem situation; • Generalize solutions and strategies to new problem situations; • Acquire confidence in using mathematics meaningfully.
Grades 9–12	The mathematics curriculum should include the refinement and extension of methods of mathematical problem solving so that all students can: • Use, with increasing confidence, problem-solving approaches to investigate and understand mathematical content; • Apply integrated mathematical problem-solving strategies to solve problems from within and outside mathematics; • Recognize and formulate problems from situations within and outside mathematics; • Apply the process of mathematical modeling to real-world problem situations.
	Mathematical connections
Grades K–4	The study of mathematics should include opportunities to make connections so that students can: • Link conceptual and procedural knowledge; • Relate various representations of concepts or procedures to one another; • Recognize relationships among different topics in mathematics; • Use mathematics in other curriculum areas; • Use mathematics in their daily lives.
Grades 5–8	The mathematics curriculum should include the investigation of mathematical connections so that students can: • See mathematics as an integrated whole; • Explore problems and describe results using graphical, numerical, physical, algebraic, and verbal mathematical models or representations; • Use a mathematical idea to further their understanding of other mathematical ideas; • Apply mathematical thinking and modeling to solve problems that arise in other disciplines; such as art, music, psychology, science, and business; • Value the role of mathematics in our culture and society.
Grades 9–12	The mathematics curriculum should include investigation of the connections and interplay among various mathematical topics and their applications so that all students can: • Recognize equivalent representations of the same concept; • Relate procedures in one representation to procedures in an equivalent representations; • Use and value the connections among mathematical topics; • Use and value the connections between mathematics and other disciplines.

Principles and Standards for School Mathematics (NCTM, 2000) is an updated version of the earlier mathematics standards. Several factors motivated this update; for example, the original consensus supporting the 1989 standards collapsed into bitter debate, some of which was about the correct interpretation of the original rhetoric and the need to solicit input from a broad range of constituencies.

Chapter 2 includes six principles—equity, curriculum, teaching, learning, assessment, and technology—that describe features of high-quality mathematics education, PreK–12. In the remaining chapters, there are five standards—number and operations, algebra, geometry, measurements, and data analysis and probability—that describe mathematical content goals. There are also five process standards—problem solving, reasoning and proof, connections, communication, and representation—for each grade band, PreK–2, 3–5, 6–8, and 9–12.

Here again, the document uses a purely mathematics lens. This is not surprising coming from the professional association of teachers of mathematics, a field that has long been in the spotlight. Apart from the math wars, assessments are regularly administered to ascertain student achievement levels in mathematics. Progress in mathematics—or the lack thereof—is often in the news.

Principles and Standards does, however, covertly acknowledge technology and engineering education. In the Technology Principle, technology—in the narrow sense of computers and calculators—is again described as a tool to enhance the teaching and learning of mathematics.

> The effective use of technology in the mathematics classroom depends on the teacher. Technology is not a panacea. As with any teaching tool, it can be used well or poorly . . . Technology not only influences how mathematics is taught and learned but also affects what is taught and when a topic appears in the curriculum. . . . (NCTM 2000, pp. 25–26)

Among the process standards, problem solving comes closest to representing an engineering concept. Students must be able to: (1) build new mathematical knowledge through problem solving, (2) solve problems that arise in mathematics and in other contexts, (3) apply and adapt a variety of appropriate strategies to solve problems, and (4) monitor and reflect on the process of mathematical problem solving. (NCTM 2000, pp. 52–54 and elaborated elsewhere in the document).

The Connections standard addresses the potential of multi-disciplinary learning. NCTM calls on teachers and students to recognize and apply mathematics in contexts outside of mathematics. "The link between mathematics and science is not only through content but also through process. The processes and content of science can inspire an approach to solving problems that applies to the study of mathematics. (NCTM 2000, p. 66).

Guiding Principles for Mathematics Curriculum and Assessment (NCTM, 2009)

With work under way to create common standards for English language arts and mathematics, NCTM recently released a document urging that they be grounded in existing work. The document concludes:

> . . . any curriculum must be linked to assessments based on standards. A curriculum should provide a rich, connected learning experience for students while adding coherence to the standards, and standards must align with the curriculum rather than be separate, long lists of learning expectations. Alignment and coherence of these three elements—curriculum, standards, and assessment—are critically important foundations of mathematics education. (NCTM, available online at *http://www.nctm.org/standards/content.aspx?id=23273*)

The predominant theme here is mastery of mathematics. No mention is made of learning through technology or engineering.

Technology and Engineering in State Standards

The No Child Left Behind Act of 2001 required that all states develop challenging academic content and student achievement standards in mathematics and science by the 2005–2006 school year. To remain eligible for federal funding, all states complied. In this section we look first at how technology and engineering fared in science standards and then how they fared in mathematics standards.

Recognizing the importance of technological literacy for all citizens, a number of states incorporated technology and engineering standards into their science standards. Massachusetts, for example, includes a K–12 strand for technology/engineering alongside (and of equal importance to) strands for physical science, life science, and Earth and space science. However, the content of technology and engineering standards included in state science frameworks overall is uneven. An analysis of the science frameworks in 49 states (Koehler et al., 2005, 2006) found that nearly all include technology in their standards, but the content of those standards is far from what it needs to be.

> . . . the nexus between engineering concepts and states science frameworks revolves around socioeconomic issues. This may be in part due to the influence of the science, technology and society (STS) movement in science education that began in the 1980s. Particularly, the socioeconomic content is described as how economics, politics and ethics coupled with technological development permeates the discipline of science. It is the means by which state science frameworks incorporate technology into their curriculums. While STS has been the traditional link between science content and technology, it is not a sufficient means to introduce engineering education and technical literacy into the high school setting. Instead, it is vital that science education focus on actual technology-based content integrated into the science curriculum as a means to promote technical literacy. (Koehler et al., 2006)

When STS standards were left out of the analysis, regional differences emerged, with states in the Northeast including the greatest number of technology and engineering standards and states in the Southeast and Mountain West region the fewest.

In addition, state mathematics frameworks are based on a different definition of "technology" than state science frameworks. In a descriptive analysis of the mathematics grade-level expectations in 42 states, the term "calculators/technology" refers to the use of electronic devices as tools to communicate concepts or solve problems (Reys, 2006). Of the 31 states that mention calculators, seven specify that students should not use them, and "all of the documents referring to calculators/technology are explicit in emphasizing that these tools do not replace the need for computational fluency" (Reys, 2006, p. 6). The authors conclude that the use of computational technology is relatively unimportant in state standards. This is a key issue in the "math wars," so it is not surprising that others disagree with this conclusion:

> One of the most debilitating trends in current state math standards is their excessive emphasis on calculators. Most standards documents call upon students to use them starting in the elementary grades, often beginning with Kindergarten. Calculators enable students to do arithmetic quickly, without thinking about the numbers involved in a calculation. For this reason, using them in a high school science class, for example, is perfectly sensible. But for elementary students, the main goal of math education is to get them to think about numbers and to learn arithmetic. Calculators defeat that

purpose. With proper restriction and guidance, calculators can play a positive role in school mathematics, but such direction is almost always missing in state standards documents. (Klein 2005, p. 1)

As the definition relates to this paper, we see that the warring parties tend to see technology as a tool for learning mathematics, rather than as a learning goal per se.

Engineering or Technology Standards?

Building on the growing use of the term "engineering" in education, Robert Wicklein (2003) proposed that focusing on engineering would be a more effective strategy for changing education than the older approach of focusing on technology for the following reasons:

- Engineering is more easily understood and valued than technology.
- Engineering elevates the field to a higher academic level.
- Engineering provides a solid framework to design curriculum.
- Engineering is ideal for integrating mathematics and science.
- Engineering provides a focused career pathway for students.

Wicklein's arguments suggest that by developing "engineering" rather than "technology" standards, we may overcome a number of barriers, such as avoiding the "vocational" label and the common misperception that technology is limited to electronic devices like computers and cell phones. This line of reasoning recently persuaded the State of Oregon to join Massachusetts and adopt "engineering design" as one of the four organizing principles of its science standards document (Oregon DOE, 2009).

While Wicklein offers thoughtful arguments, the jury is still out on whether "technology" or "engineering" is the better term from a strategic point of view. Both New Hampshire and Washington State decided to include a strong component of engineering in their standards, but both preferred the term "technological design" rather than "engineering design" because teachers fear engineering as a subject they may not be able to comprehend, but are comfortable with the pairing of terms "science and technology." Also, a new framework for a national test of technological literacy beginning in 2012 is currently being developed (NAGB, in press).

In Search of an Effective Strategy

As illustrated in the previous section, the current science standards documents include technology and engineering, albeit with different definitions of the terms. However, most practitioners have ignored those standards and focused instead on traditional science disciplines. Mathematics standards use an even narrower definition of "technology" as limited to computational tools, and there are vigorous debates in the mathematics community about whether or not to include technology at all.

For the next attempt at integrating technology and engineering standards into mainstream subject standards to be more successful, we must pay more attention to terms and definitions. Wicklein suggests using "engineering" as a more promising strategy than "technology." Although there are misunderstandings about both terms, we agree that the people's conceptions about engineering are probably narrower than their conceptions of technology. However, this suggests that an effective strategy must develop clear definitions of both terms with relevant examples.

A second strategy would be to conduct case studies of successful implementations of engineering standards. For example, the State of Massachusetts has a network of school district teams to help implement state technology/engineering standards at the district level. These teams share information about their challenges and successes and borrow ideas from each other. A recently developed curriculum, *Engineering is Elementary*, provides materials that can be integrated with reading and social studies lessons at the elementary level, along with science learning activities. Several evaluation studies of this curriculum have been conducted. New Jersey has had a very active professional development program for teachers for several years focused on technological design. Project Lead the Way is a rigorous high school engineering program that has been implemented in more than 1,000 high schools nationwide. These and other educational projects should be reviewed for lessons on integrating engineering into the curriculum for all students and on how standards can support those efforts.

A third strategy would be to develop a small set of big ideas that we want students to understand at a deep level, to remember for many years after leaving high school, and to find useful in everyday life. These big ideas would provide guidelines for deciding what to include and what to exclude from the standards. The practice of starting with big ideas to establish a framework is not new (McCarthy and Comfort, 1993). However, it has gained recent attention in two influential publications from the National Research Council (Duschl et al., 2007; Michaels et al., 2008). To avoid repeating past mistakes, it will be important that the big ideas in engineering be complementary to core subjects so practitioners view them as central ideas and not add-ons. For example, engineering can be used to illustrate why science is important and how engineering design problems can help students understand and apply physical, life, Earth and space science concepts. Engineering problems can also engage students in solving problems that can sharpen their mathematical abilities.

Establishing a common language for science and mathematics educators when discussing engineering would be challenging, but it could be done. The next step would be to vet the list of big ideas, either by consulting with engineers, educators, and other experts, researching the literature on educational research, or making international comparisons.

Table 6 offers a recommendation for big ideas in three dimensions of engineering education: critical *knowledge* about the engineering design process, *skill sets* that enable students to apply the process, and *habits of mind* that frame the way students approach problematic situations. The meaning of these big ideas and how they might play out at the elementary, middle school, and high school levels is elaborated in Appendix B, p. 136.

Table 6. A Vision of Engineering Standards in Terms of Big Ideas

Knowledge	1. Engineering design is an approach to solving problems or achieving goals.
	2. Technology is a fundamental attribute of human culture.
	3. Science and engineering differ in terms of goals, processes, and products.
Skills	4. Designing under constraint.
	5. Using tools and materials.
	6. Mathematical reasoning.
Habits of Mind	7. Systems thinking.
	8. Desire to encourage and support effective teamwork.
	9. Concern for the societal and environmental impacts of technology.

Engineering standards based on a big ideas like these could be more concise and focused than past standards and could emphasize connections and distinctions among fields of science, technology, engineering, and mathematics.

Conclusion

The preliminary ideas offered here do not even begin to address the deeper issues of implementation. In Massachusetts, which enacted the strongest set of technology and engineering standards in the nation in 2001, considerable progress has been made in many school districts to implement the standards. However, change at the classroom level has required significant time and funding from a number of governmental and private organizations in the state.

Although educational systems have a great deal of inertia, they can be moved. Recent discussions about accountability in the forthcoming reauthorization of the Elementary and Secondary Education Act have suggested the need for ". . . incorporating indicators of the many fields of knowledge and skills that young people need to be successful." (A Broader, Bolder Approach, available on-line at *http://www.boldapproach.org/report_20090625.html*) If enacted into law, this philosophy may help motivate change as well.

We are optimistic that, if a clear, concise vision for engineering education can be developed and integrated into the fabric of state standards in the core subjects of science and mathematics, then implementation of engineering education will begin to take hold.

References

AAAS (1990). *Science for All Americans: A Project 2061 Report.* American Association for the Advancement of Science, Project 2061. New York, NY: Oxford University Press.

AAAS (1993). *Benchmarks for Science Literacy.* American Association for the Advancement of Science, Project 2061. New York, NY: Oxford University Press.

Beatty, Alexandra, Rapporteur (2008). *Common Standards for K–12 Education?: Considering the Evidence:* Summary of a Workshop Series, Committee on State Standards in Education: A Workshop Series, National Research Council. Washington, DC: National Academies Press.

Duschl, R.A., Schweingruber, H.A., and Shouse, A.W., eds. (2007). *Taking Science to School: Learning and Teaching Science in Grades K–8.* National Research Council. Washington, DC: National Academies Press.

Foecke, H. A. (1970). "Engineering in the Humanistic Tradition," *Impact of Science on Society*, vol. XX, no. 2.

Foecke, Harold A. (1995). "Fifty Years of UNESCO Leadership in Science and Technology Education," UNESCO 50 Years for Education, CD-ROM.

Hudson, S., McMahon, K., and Overstreet, C. (2002). The 2000 National Survey of Science and Mathematics Education: Compendium of Tables. Chapel Hill, NC: Horizon Research, Inc.

ITEA (2000). *Standards for Technological Literacy: Content for the Study of Technology.* International Technology Education Association and National Academy of Engineering. Reston, VA: International Technology Education Association.

Klein, D., et al. (2005). *The State of State Math Standards.* Available online at http://www.edexcellence.net/detail/news.cfm?news_id=338.

Koehler, C., Faraclas, E., Giblin, D., Kazerounian, K., and Moss, D. (2006). Are concepts of technical & engineering literacy included in state curriculum standards? A regional overview of the nexus between technical & engineering literacy and state science frameworks. *Proceedings of 2006 ASEE Annual Conference and Exposition,* Chicago, IL, Paper No. 2006-1510, June 18-21.

Koehler, C., Faraclas, E., Sanchez, S., Latif, S.K., and Kazerounian, K. (2005). Engineering frameworks for a high school setting: Guidelines for technical literacy for high school students. *Proceedings of 2005 ASEE Annual Conference and Exposition.*

Layton, D. (1993). *Technology's Challenge to Science Education: Cathedral, Quarry, or Company Store?* Philadelphia: Open University Press.

MA DOE (2001, 2006). *Massachusetts Science and Technology/Engineering Curriculum Framework.* Malden, MA: Massachusetts Department of Education. Available online at http://www.doe.mass.edu/frameworks/scitech/1006.pdf.

McCarthy, J. and Comfort, K. (1993). *What's the Big Idea? An Assessment Framework for CLAS Science Assessment.* Sacramento, CA: California Department of Education.

McNeil, Michelle (2009). "Forty-Six States Commit to Common Standards Push." Education Week, June 1, 2009. Available online at http://www.edweek.org.

Michaels, S., Shouse, A.W., and Schweingruber, H.A. (2008). In *Ready, Set, Science!: Putting Research to Work in K–8 Science Classrooms.* Washington, DC: National Academies Press.

NAGB (In Press). *Technology Framework for the 2009 National Assessment of Educational Progress.* National Assessment Governing Board. Washington, DC: U.S. Government Printing Office.

NAGB (2008). *Science Framework for the 2009 National Assessment of Educational Progress.* National Assessment Governing Board. Washington, DC: U.S. Government Printing Office.

NCTM (1980). NCTM, 1980, *An Agenda for Action: Recommendations for School Mathematics of the 1980s.* National Council of Teachers of Mathematics. Reston, VA: NCTM.

NCTM (1989). *Curriculum and Evaluation Standards for School Mathematics.* National Council of Teachers of Mathematics. Reston, VA: NCTM.

NCTM (2000). *Principles and Standards for School Mathematics.* National Council of Teachers of Mathematics. Reston, VA: NCTM.

NCTM (2008). *The Role of Technology in the Teaching and Learning of Mathematics.* Online at http://www.nctm.org/about/content.aspx?id=14233.

NRC (National Research Council) (1996). *National Science Education Standards.* Washington, DC: National Academy Press.

NRC (2005). *Rising above the Gathering Storm: Energizing and Employing America for a Brighter Economic Future.* National Research Council. Washington DC: National Academies Press.

ODE (2009). Science Content Standards Revision Draft. Oregon Department of Education. Available online at: http://www.ode.state.or.us/search/page/?=2560

Reys, B., ed. (2006). *The Intended Curriculum as Represented in State-Level Curriculum Standards: Consensus or Confusion?* Charlotte, NC: Information Age Publishing.

UNESCO (United Nations Educational, Scientific, and Cultural Organization) (1986–2003). *Innovations in Science and Technology Education.* Volumes I–VIII. Paris: UNESCO Publishing.

Wicklein, R. (2003). Five good reasons for engineering as THE focus for technology education. Athens: University of Georgia. Available online at: http://www.uga.edu/teched/conf/wick_engr.pdf.

Appendix A

The *2000 National Survey of Science and Mathematics Education*, by Susan B. Hudson, Kelly C. McMahon, and Christina M. Overstreet, provides a wealth of data, based on responses from 5,765 science and mathematics teachers across the United States (Hudson, 2002). This volume contains tables of frequencies for each item on the questionnaire, copies of the instruments, and details on data collection and analysis. Results are available online at: *http://2000survey.horizon-research.com/reports/tables.php*.

	Mathematics Standards How familiar are you with the NCTM *Standards*?
Grades K–4	38% of respondents "Not at all familiar" 31% of respondents "Somewhat familiar" 21% of respondents "Fairly familiar" 10% of respondents "Very familiar"
Grades 5–8	27% of respondents "Not at all familiar" 24% of respondents "Somewhat familiar" 30% of respondents "Fairly familiar" 19% of respondents "Very familiar"
Grades 9–12	15% of respondents "Not at all familiar" 31% of respondents "Somewhat familiar" 35% of respondents "Fairly familiar" 19% of respondents "Very familiar"
	2a. How familiar are you with the *National Science Education Standards*, published by the National Research Council?
Grades K–4	67% of respondents "Not at all familiar" 22% of respondents "Somewhat familiar" 9% of respondents "Fairly familiar" 2% of respondents "Very familiar"
Grades 5–8	42% of respondents "Not at all familiar" 31% of respondents "Somewhat familiar 19% of respondents "Fairly familiar" 8% of respondents "Very familiar"
Grades 9–12	37% of respondents "Not at all familiar" 34% of respondents "Somewhat familiar" 18% of respondents "Fairly familiar" 10% of respondents "Very familiar"

Appendix B: DRAFT
A Vision of Engineering Standards in Terms of Big Ideas

Cary Sneider, Associate Research Professor, Portland State University
Based on earlier work at the Museum of Science, Boston

One way of developing standards that are clear, coherent, focused, and rigorous is to first identify a small set of big ideas that we want students to understand at a deep level, to remember for many years after leaving high school, and to find useful in their everyday lives. These big ideas would provide a means of deciding what to include and what to exclude from the standards. The following table is a suggested list of big ideas in three dimensions of engineering education: critical *knowledge* about the engineering design process, *skill sets* that enable students to apply the process, and *habits of mind* that frame the way students approach problematic situations.

Knowledge	1. Engineering design is an approach to solving problems or achieving goals.
	2. Technology is a fundamental attribute of human culture
	3. Science and engineering differ in terms of goals, processes, and products.
Skill Sets	4. Designing under constraint.
	5. Using tools and materials.
	6. Mathematical reasoning.
Habits of Mind	7. Systems thinking.
	8. Desire to encourage and support effective teamwork.
	9. Concern for the societal and environmental impacts of technology.

In the remainder of this appendix, we list learning expectations for the elementary, middle, and high school levels for each big idea, skill set, and habit of mind. We use the term *benchmarks* to denote what students should know and be able to do at the 5th, 8th, and 12th grade levels, provided they have had adequate opportunities to learn the engineering design process. These learning expectations are based on prior national standards (NSES, *Benchmarks,* and STL), and our own experience in developing and evaluating K–12 curriculum materials in technology and engineering.

Knowledge

Three big ideas characterize what students need to know about the engineering design process: (1) engineering design is an approach to defining and solving problems; (2) technology is a fundamental attribute of human culture; and (3) engineering and science are different but mutually reinforcing endeavors. Learning expectations for each of these big ideas are listed below.

1. Engineering design is an approach to solving problems or achieving goals. Problems and goals can be defined so they can be tackled systematically and satisfying solutions can be found.

   Grades K–5: Elementary school children understand that everyone can design a solution to a problem. Given a problem statement, they can ask questions to clarify the problem and learn what others have done, imagine what some solutions might be, create a plan and test a possible solution, then improve the design and communicate it others.

Grades 5–8: At the middle school level students can more thoroughly describe how the engineering design process would be applied to a problem situation. They can describe steps that can be performed in different sequences and repeated as needed. Although there are slightly different descriptions of the design process in the literature, most converge on a set of steps like the following: (1) define the problem, (2) research how others have solved it, (3) generate several alternative solutions, (4) select the most promising solution, (5) make a prototype, (6) test and evaluate it, (7) communicate the results, (8) redesign based on feedback.

Grades 9–12: When asked to describe technologies around them, high school students recognize that almost everything that they see, touch, hear, or otherwise experience has been designed by people using the engineering design process. One way of demonstrating this knowledge is by "reverse engineering" an everyday example of technology. They also understand that the engineering design process is a highly flexible approach to recognizing, defining, and solving problems or to meeting human needs or desires.

2. Technology is a fundamental attribute of human culture. We define human cultures largely in terms of the technologies people in those cultures engineer and use.

Grades K–5: At the elementary level students can distinguish things found in nature from things that are made by people. They can also give examples of how naturally occurring materials such as wood, clay, cotton, and animal skins may be processed or combined with other materials to change their properties in order to solve human problems and enhance the quality of life.

Grades 5–8: Middle school students can explain how technologies such as spear points, grinding bowls, and pottery provide evidence of how people who lived long ago solved problems, how they must have lived, and even something of their creativity and sense of aesthetics. They can give examples of historical periods that have been named for the dominant technology, such as the Iron Age, the Bronze Age, or the Industrial Revolution. They can also give examples of the vast number and variety of technologies that pervade modern society, as well as technologies that are particular to their own cultural communities.

Grades 9–12: High school students can cite some evidence in support of the statement that "As long as there have been people, there has been technology." They can also cite evidence that technology has been a powerful force in the development of civilization by giving examples of how technology has shaped values, commerce, language, and the arts. High school students should also be able to describe the rapid pace of technological change in their own era, as well as modern civilization's dependence on technological systems, such as the electrical power grid, transportation systems, and food production and distribution systems.

3. Science and engineering differ in terms of goals, processes, and products. Science is a means of learning about the natural world, while engineering is a process for changing it. Technological advances may enable new scientific discoveries, while scientific understanding sometimes results in new or improved technologies.

Grades K–5: Students are able to distinguish the questioning, observation, and experimentation process of scientific inquiry from the problem-solving process of engineering design. They can give examples of how a scientist might go about studying the life cycle of a butterfly and how an engineer might go about designing a better car. They can also give examples of how engineers apply science in their work and how scientists rely on technologies developed by engineers.

Grades 5–8: Middle school students can explain the differences in goals, processes, and products of scientists and engineers. They can also give examples of why engineering is essential to science (e.g. for gaining access to outer space, for observing very small or very distant objects) and why science is essential to engineering (e.g., for helping engineers understand why things work, such as how airplanes fly, so that they can be improved). They can also describe a wide variety of engineering professions and recognize that men and women from different ethnic and cultural backgrounds have chosen to be engineers.

Grades 9–12: Students at the high school level will be able to express a richer sense of the relationships linking technology and science. They can give examples of how technological problems sometimes create a demand for new scientific knowledge and how new technologies make it possible for scientists to extend their research in new ways or to undertake entirely new lines of research. Most important, they can cite modern examples of the complementary relationship between science and technology in fields such as medical research and nanotechnology, and they can describe the educational pathway that individuals must follow if they choose to pursue careers in science or engineering.

Skill Sets

Although many skills contribute to a person's capability to engage in engineering design, we have identified the following skill sets as the most essential: (4) designing under constraint; (5) using tools and materials; and (6) mathematical reasoning. Although this brief section does not define levels of skill performance, a major goal of this study will be to specify skill levels and figure out how teachers can determine their students' skill levels through embedded assessments.

4. Designing under constraint is the ability to apply all of the steps of the engineering design process in real-world contexts.

Grades K–4: Elementary school students can learn that the problem-definition phase of engineering design includes identifying desired characteristics of the solution (criteria), as well as limits (constraints). Young children can learn about constraints such as safety, time, cost, school policy, space, availability of materials, and other realities that restrict possible solutions. Teachers can point out that adults also face constraints when they design things and that the real challenge, for adults and children, is to devise solutions that achieve good results in spite of the restrictions. However, elementary students should not be faced with problems that involve too many variables at one time. When generating possible solutions young children have a tendency to go with their first idea. Learning to suspend judgment until other ideas for solving a problem have been generated can be very challenging for elementary students but is a very important element of the decision-making process.

Grades 5–8: Middle school students should develop skill in defining problems in which there may be competing interests and values. They should learn to use brainstorming as a means of generating diverse solutions and to develop analytical tools for choosing among possible ideas, even when the data are unclear or incomplete. One of the most important tools they should learn to use is the idea of trade-offs—designs that are best in one respect (safety or ease of use, for example) but may be inferior in other ways (cost or appearance). The students should be able to justify decisions in terms of trade-offs and acknowledge that other individuals may have different, also justifiable solutions to the same problem. Middle school students should also have experience in testing prototypes as a way of transforming ideas into practical solutions. Finally, they should have experiences in which they communicate their ideas using drawings and simple models, receive feedback on their ideas, and then redesign their solutions in light of that feedback.

Grades 9–12: High school students should have opportunities to define solvable problems, with clearly identified criteria and constraints, in situations that may at first seem chaotic. Once a solvable problem is defined and the students have brainstormed alternative solutions, they should be able to make decisions about which solutions are best in light of uncertain or partial data. Good engineering design is distinguished by the ability to make the best possible decision in light of real-world uncertainties. The use of a Pugh chart is a helpful analytic tool for comparing various solutions against criteria and constraints. High school students should also be more sophisticated than middle school students in their ability to build and test prototypes or simulate technological systems to come up with the best possible solution.

5. Using tools and materials involves the selection, testing, and use of appropriate tools and materials to solve a problem or meet a human need.

Grades K–5: In early years, students develop simple skills using tools and materials, such as how to measure, cut, connect, switch, turn on and off, pour, hold, tie, and hook. Beginning with simple instruments, students can use rulers to measure the length, height, and depth of objects and materials; thermometers to measure temperature; watches to measure time; beam balances and spring scales to measure weight and force; magnifiers to observe objects and organisms; and microscopes to observe the finer details of plants, animals, rocks, and other materials. Children should also develop skills in selecting among different materials to choose those most useful for a given purpose.

Grades 5–8: Middle school students should have a broad view of Earth materials such as solid rocks and soils, water in the forms liquid and ice, and the gases in the atmosphere. These varied materials have different physical and chemical properties, which make them useful in different ways, for example, as building materials, as sources of fuel, or for growing the plants we use as food. The choice of materials for a job depends on their properties and on how they interact with other materials. Similarly, the usefulness of some manufactured parts of an object depends on how well the parts fit together. Middle school students should also exhibit capabilities in the use of computers and calculators for solving problems.

Grades 9–12: In addition to the above experiences with tools and materials, high school students should have opportunities to illustrate their ideas through engineering drawings and computer aided design (CAD) systems, if possible. They should also have opportunities to use a variety of tools and materials to construct prototypes of their own design and to test the design concept by observing its function in representative situations so that it can be redesigned for manufacturing.

6. Mathematical reasoning involves using fundamental mathematical skills to solve problems or build prototypes.

Grades K–5: Young children should develop the capability of making measurements to answer questions about objects such as "How tall is it?" "How much does it hold?" "How big is it?" They should also encounter situations in which they need to use simple arithmetic operations to solve problems related to a design challenge.

Grades 5–8: At the middle school level students can make more varied and precise measurements as well as more challenging estimates. They are also capable of understanding more abstract measurement concepts, such as the idea of a "measurement unit," the conversion of units from one system to another, and the limitations of measurements made with different instruments. Negative numbers, fractions, and decimals can now be used in the service of solving problems. Students should demonstrate their capability not only to carry out operations accurately, but also to choose the appropriate operation and/or level of estimation or precision of measurement for a given situation.

Grades 9–12: While high school students can be expected to bring additional skills (algebra, geometry, trigonometry and possibly elementary calculus) to the engineering design process, the major focus should be on determining whether or not students have developed advanced skills in determining the most appropriate operations to address various steps of the process—defining problems quantitatively, creating engineering drawings with scale factors, using tools to accurately measure materials, setting up a testing apparatus that allows for quantitative comparisons of different materials and structures, etc.

Habits of Mind

The engineering design requires a different mind set from the mind set appropriate to science, mathematics, or any other academic field. We've divided these "habits of mind" into three areas: (7) systems thinking; (8) teamwork; and (9) societal and environmental impacts of technology.

7. Systems thinking is a way of approaching problems with a recognition that all technologies are systems of interacting parts that are, in turn, embedded in larger systems. While it may be argued that systems thinking is both a big idea and a skill set, we have chosen to list it as a habit of mind to emphasize that systems thinking is—more importantly—a worldview.

> **Grades K–5:** Young children can learn that things consist of interacting parts. Our bodies, for example, are natural systems that contain many different parts that act together to keep us alive and active. Children should consider many other systems as well, both technological and natural. In addition, young children can learn that everything is connected to everything else, so damage to one part of a system may affect the function of the system as a whole. Food webs are frequently presented to elementary students as systems, but many other examples should also be presented.

> **Grades 5–8:** Middle school students can learn that complex technological systems require control mechanisms. The essence of control is comparing information about what is happening to what people want to happen and then making appropriate adjustments. This procedure requires sensing information, processing it, and making changes. The common thermostat can serve as a model for control mechanisms. Students should explore how controls work in various kinds of systems—machines, athletic contests, politics, the human body, and so on. Students should also try to invent control mechanisms that they can actually put into operation. As a habit of mind, understanding systems at the middle school level means that whenever students approach a new problem they consider the system as a whole, how it functions, and how it is controlled.

> **Grades 9–12:** High school students should have opportunities to explore more complex technological systems, including how technologies interact with social and cultural systems. They should be aware that complex systems have layers of controls. Some controls operate particular parts of the system, and some control other controls. Even fully automatic systems require human control at some point. High school students should also be able to analyze technological systems using the ideas of universal design and life cycle analysis. The universal design model involves analysis of goals, inputs and outputs, internal processes, feedback, and control. Life cycle analysis of a device or process involves how it will be manufactured, operated, maintained, replaced, and disposed of and who will sell, operate, and take care of it. As a habit of mind, students are able to break out of the narrow definition of a problem and reflect on the relevant systems and how they affect, and in turn are affected by, new and improved technologies.

8. The desire to encourage and support effective teamwork is a hallmark of capable engineering work, since no single individual is likely to bring to a problem situation all of the necessary knowledge and skills for a good solution.

> **Grades K–5:** A predisposition to work with others and contribute effectively on a team takes many years to develop, preferably beginning in elementary school. In the early elementary years it is challenging for students to consider other students' ideas, especially if they conflict with their own ideas. By the end of fifth grade students should be able to do this well and to reflect what they like about working on teams and what conflicts that they try to avoid. They should also be aware that

their own teams are like those of scientists and engineers, in that individuals with different capabilities and talents combine their efforts to arrive at a better solution as a team than they could as individuals.

Grades 5–8: Middle school students should be aware that most of the work of engineers involves working as a member of a team. In addition, one of the advantages of teams is that they may include a wide diversity of talents and points of view from women and men of various social and ethnic backgrounds with different interests, capabilities, and motivations. Evidence of effective teamwork might include full participation with other students on teams, the ability to communicate ideas clearly, but also active listening to teammates and a willingness to work with widely diverse individuals.

Grades 9–12: High school students should move to higher levels of critical and creative thinking through progressively more demanding design and technology teamwork. In addition to team-building skills mentioned above, high school students should show evidence that they recognize the advantages of the combination of teamwork and individual effort, that they focus on the quality of work by the entire team, and that they are willing to engage and assist weaker members of their team.

9. Concern for the societal and environmental impacts of technology involves personal values as well as knowledge and skills.

Grades K–5: Elementary school students are capable of realizing that because of our ability to invent tools, materials, and processes, we humans have an enormous effect on the lives of other living things. New or improved technologies can have both positive and negative impacts. Consequently, decisions involving technology should be made with possible societal and environmental impacts in mind.

Grades 5–8: At the middle school level students should show evidence of a more sophisticated understanding of the pros and cons of technological changes. On the positive side, transportation, communications, nutrition, sanitation, health care, entertainment, and other technologies give large numbers of people today the goods and services that once were luxuries enjoyed only by the wealthy. However, these benefits are not equally available to everyone. Furthermore, technological changes often have side effects that were not anticipated. For example, the first pioneering engineers who developed automobiles did not realize that this invention would cause tens of thousands of deaths per year as the speed of cars increased. Students' decision-making should show evidence that they are attempting to take possible societal and environmental impacts into account.

Grades 9–12: High school students should be able to conduct risk analyses of technological innovations to minimize the likelihood of unwanted side effects of a new technology by considering such questions as: What alternative ways are there to achieve the same ends, and how do the alternatives compare to the plan being put forward? Who benefits and who suffers? What are the financial and social costs, do they change over time, and who bears them? What are the risks associated with using (or not using) the new technology, how serious are they, and who is in jeopardy? What human, material, and energy resources will be needed to build, install, operate, maintain, and replace the new technology, and where will they come from? How will the new technology and its waste products be disposed of and at what cost? Students should also be aware that risk can be reduced in a variety of ways: overdesign, redundancy, fail-safe designs, more research ahead of time, more controls, etc. They should also come to recognize that the cost of such precautions may become prohibitive.

Appendix C

Workshop on Standards for K–12 Engineering Education

July 8–9, 2009

National Academy of Engineering
Keck Center of the National Academies
500 5th St., NW
Washington, D.C.

Day 1: July 8

8:30 a.m.   **Welcome, Goals for the Day, and Introductions**
Bob White, Carnegie Mellon University (emeritus) and Chair
Committee on K–12 Engineering Standards

Setting the Context

8:45 a.m.   **The Status of K–12 Engineering Education in the United States:**
Upcoming Report from the National Academies
Greg Pearson, Study Director
NAE/NRC Committee on K–12 Engineering Education

9:00 a.m.   **Opportunities and Barriers to Developing Standards for K–12 Engineering**
Rodger Bybee, Bybee Consulting

9:30 a.m.   **Discussion**
Committee and Guests

10:00 a.m.   **Break**

Need, Effectiveness, and Unintended Consequences

10:15 a.m.   **An Industry View on Standards for K–12 Engineering**
Ray Morrison, Lockheed Martin (ret.)
and Ray Haynes, Northrop Grumman, ASEE Corporate Member Council

Impact of Standards: Reflections on a Paper by Harris and Goertz
Committee Panel: Jim Spohrer, IBM Almaden Research Center; Mario Godoy-Gonzalez, Royal High School, Royal, Washington; and Elizabeth Stage, Lawrence Hall of Science

The Unintended Consequences of Standards
*Deborah Meier, NYU

11:15 a.m.   **Moderated Discussion: Are Standards for K–12 Engineering a Good Idea, Are They Feasible?**
Committee, Presenters, and Guests
Moderator: TBD

12:00 p.m.   **Lunch**

Luncheon Speaker: *Steve Robinson, Special Advisor to the Secretary, U.S. Department of Education, "K–12 STEM Education and Standards: A View from the New Administration"*

Engineering in Existing K–12 Standards

1:00 p.m.   **Engineering Concepts and Skills in State K–12 Curriculum Frameworks**

The Case of Massachusetts
Jake Foster, Massachusetts Department of Elementary and Secondary Education

The Case of New Jersey
Beth McGrath, Stevens Institute of Technology

The Case of Minnesota
*Clark Erickson, Minnesota Department of Education (ret.)

2:00 p.m.   **Engineering-Related Concepts and Skills in National K–12Standards Documents for Science, Mathematics, and Technology Education**
Cary Sneider, Boston Museum of Science (ret.)
and Linda Rosen (Committee Member), Education and Management Innovations

2:30 p.m.   **Q&A with Committee**

* Participating by telephone.

3:00 p.m.   **Break**

<u>Other Perspectives</u>

3:15 p.m.   **Comments from Engineering and Business**

- **American Society for Engineering Education**
  - **Division on K–12 & Pre-College Engineering:** *Elizabeth Parry, North Carolina State University College of Engineering*
  - **Engineering Deans Council:** *Nicholas Altiero, Tulane University*
- **Business Higher Education Forum:** *Chris Roe*
- **Business Roundtable:** *Susan Traiman*

4:00 p.m.   **Q&A with Committee**

4:30 p.m.   **Comments from Educators**

Moderated panel:

- *Steve Wagner, engineering teacher, Highland Springs High School, Virginia*
- *Robert Willis, biology teacher, Ballou High School, Washington, D.C.*
- *Dayo Akinsheye, principal, Marie H. Reed Community Learning Center, Washington, D.C.*
- *Gladys Whitehead, director of curriculum and instruction, Prince Georges County Public Schools, Maryland*

5:30 p.m.   **Adjourn**

Workshop on Standards for K–12 Engineering Education

July 8–9, 2009
National Academy of Engineering
Keck Center of the National Academies
Washington, D.C.

<u>Day 2: July 9</u>

8:30 a.m.   **Welcome and Plans for the Day**
Bob White, Carnegie Mellon University (emeritus) and Committee Chair

<u>Content for K–12 Engineering Standards</u>

8:45 a.m.   **Identification of Core Engineering Knowledge at the High School Level: Report of a Study**
Rod Custer, Jenny Daugherty, and Joe Meyer, Illinois State University (National Center for Engineering and Technology Education)

Engineering and the ITEA Standards for Technological Literacy: History and Status
Kendall Starkweather, International Technology Education Association

9:45 a.m.   **Q&A with Committee**

10:15 a.m.   **Break**

<u>"Standards 2.0": New Models for the New Century</u>

10:30 a.m.   **Alternatives to Traditional Content Standards: Discussion of Framing Paper by Committee Member Jim Rutherford**
Summary of Paper: Christine Cunningham, Committee
Discussants: Jan Morrison, TIES
Torrence Robinson, Texas Instruments
Gerhard Salinger, NSF
Senta Raizen (invited), WestEd

11:15 a.m.   **Committee Discussion**

11:30 a.m.   **Fewer Concepts, Greater Depth**

- **NCTM "Focal Points" Project,** *Jim Rubillo, National Council of Teachers of Mathematics*

- **NSTA "Science Anchors" Project,** *Francis Eberle, National Science Teachers Association*

12:15 p.m.   **Q&A with Committee**

12:30 p.m.   **Lunch**

1:15 p.m.   **Focus on College and Workplace Readiness**

- **American Diploma Project,** *Jean Slattery, Achieve, Inc.*
- ****Partnership for 21st Century Skills,** *Valerie Greenhill, e-Luminate Group*
- **Career Clusters,** *Kim Green, National Association of State Directors of Career Technical Education Consortium*

2:15 p.m.   **Creating Consistency and Rigor**

- **Council of Chief State School Officers—National Governors Association Common Standards Initiative,** *Scott Montgomery, CCSSO*

2:45 p.m.   **Q&A with Committee**

3:00 p.m.   **Break**

3:15 p.m.   **Stakeholder Comment Session**

[NOTE: A variety of organizations will be invited to provide brief (5 minutes) comments for the committee's consideration. Those who cannot attend the workshop in person may submit written comments via e-mail. Questions that might guide this input are attached as an annex to this agenda.]

4:00 p.m.   **Final Thoughts and Next Steps**
Bob White and Committee

4:15 p.m.   **Adjourn**

** Participating by videoconference.

ANNEX

<u>Questions to Guide Input for "Stakeholder Comment Session," July 9</u>

1. To the extent that you are aware of such efforts, in general, do you think teaching engineering in K–12 schools is a good idea or not, and why?

2. Many areas of education (e.g., mathematics, science, history, geography) have developed content standards that suggest what K–12 students should know and be able to do at different points in their school careers. No such standards exist for engineering.

   a. Would such standards for engineering be a good idea or not, and why?
   b. What alternatives to traditional standards might help bring consistency and coherence to K–12 engineering education?

3. What other advice or comments, if any, do you have for the committee?